THE
COURAGE
TO LIVE

MARSHA MANSOUR

Published by

LIFEBRIDGE
BOOKS
P.O. BOX 49428
CHARLOTTE, NC 28277

DEDICATION

When I reflect on this title, "The Courage to Live," the people that swell up in my heart are my amazing parents, Mofid and Madeline Mansour. They are the definition for courage. They came to this country led of the Lord with no support, employment, or encouragement. They arrived with nothing except their bags and their three year old baby (me)—and built everything they had with their own hands.

My parents faced countless trials, but with each one they stood tall, and the Lord made them the head and not the tail. Everything that I am starts and finishes with them. They are the most godly, loving and generous people, and I am blessed to call them my parents! This book is a testimony to their lives. They inspire me every day.

CONTENTS

INTRODUCTION

If this book makes you feel uncomfortable with the status quo, that is my intention.

You and I were never placed on this planet to live an ordinary, humdrum existence—waking up, trudging to work, coming home, sleeping, and repeating the routine all over again.

On these pages you will be challenged to have the courage to move beyond just breathing, and truly start living.

- It takes courage to rise above average.
- It takes courage to awaken to life.
- It takes courage to open your eyes to God's purpose.
- It takes courage to align your life with the supernatural.
- It takes courage to fulfill your destiny.

As you will discover, God has a divine plan for your life. And with this plan He will also provide you with power, purpose, and protection. I pray these words will cause you to welcome a divine transformation in your life today. May your hunger for the Lord increase with such intensity that you become unstoppable in the work of the kingdom.

If you are ready to align yourself with God's Spirit and allow Christ to be formed in you, read on.

I am thrilled that you have joined me on this journey and, with God's help, you will truly find *The Courage to Live!*

– *Marsha Mofid Mansour*

CHAPTER 1

ARE YOU LIVING OR JUST BREATHING?

When I bump into a believer and ask, "How are you doing?" I expect a positive reply.

Far too often, however, the response is a lackluster, "Oh, I'm okay."

Such a reaction bothers me because you and I were placed on this earth to walk in abundance and live a victorious life. We were never meant just to breathe and hopefully, somehow, someway, struggle through each day. That wasn't the Creator's purpose.

The moment you gave your heart to Jesus, new life began to flow out of you. Yet there are constant forces at play attempting to squelch the precious gift you have been given.

There are few things worse than a powerless saint or a lethargic, comatose Christian. Those are actually contradictions of terms, because Jesus Himself is life—and everything He touches comes alive.

LIVING WATER

One of my favorite stories of Christ's ministry on earth is the encounter He had with the woman of Samaria who came to draw water at a well.

Jesus was standing there alone when she arrived on the scene, and He politely said to her, *"Give Me a drink"* (John 4:7)—because His disciples had gone into the city to buy food.

The woman was quite taken back, and asked Jesus, *"How is it that you being a Jew ask a drink of me? A Samaritan woman?"* (verse 9). The Jews, you see, had no dealings with Samaria.

Jesus answered her with these words: *"If you knew the gift of God, and who it is who says to you, 'Give Me a drink,' you would have asked Him, and He would have given you living water"* (verse 10).

The Samaritan woman responded, *"Sir, You have nothing to draw with, and the well is deep. Where then do You get that living water? Are You greater than our father Jacob, who gave us the well, and drank from it himself, as well as his sons and his livestock?"* (verses 11-12).

Then Jesus made one of the most profound statements recorded in the Bible. He answered, *"Whoever drinks of this water will thirst again, but whoever drinks of the water that I shall give him will never thirst"* (verses 13-14).

What a picture! We can almost visualize the pure, flowing water bubbling up from that well. It is a portrayal of life—our life!

It is the Lord's deep desire for you to not merely survive, but to live your days on earth with overflowing favor.

Are there hindrances along the way? Absolutely. Jesus tells us, *"The thief does not come except to steal, and to kill, and to destroy, I have come that they may have life, and that they may have it more abundantly"* (John 10:10).

What does Satan try to rob you of? Your very *life*—and every component of your life! In truth, we face three enemies: the world, the flesh, and the devil.

You may ask, "My flesh?" Certainly.

When you were born again, your spirit was saved, but your heart and mind didn't get the memo! They are very *un*-saved, and are constantly at war with your spirit. They continually battle your living water

11

because their purpose is to halt the flow. That's what they do.

THREE LIFE-CHANGING KEYS

If you long for a brand new breath of life and to experience refreshing, abundant water, let me give you three essential keys:

Key #1: Walk and Live in the Word of God

God's written Word, the Bread of Life, should be our diet 24 hours a day.

Scripture declares, *"For the word of God is living and powerful, and sharper than any two-edged sword, piercing even to the division of soul and spirit, and of joints and marrow, and is a discerner of the thoughts and intents of the heart"* (Hebrews 4:12).

How is it possible to live in the Word?

- Read it.
- Meditate on it.
- Pray it.
- Speak it—again, again, and again!

If you want power when you pray to your heavenly Father, avoid using only your limited vocabulary, use His Word. If you want liberty in your life, don't just rely on *your* words, speak *His* Word!

In our day-to-day, fast-paced world, we are quick to quote statistics and listen to doctors and specialists, yet we often forget that we have access to the best resource and the Greatest Specialist known to man— simply by opening the pages of Scripture.

ANDY'S URGENT CALL

For several years I was a youth pastor and called the young people under my care my "sons" and "daughters."

One of these "sons," named Andy, was accepted at West Point. While a cadet there, however, he found himself in a bit of trouble. At a military college, they don't look too favorably on pranks.

Andy is a jokester, and he pulled a stunt that he shouldn't have. To him it wasn't a big deal, but those in authority were ready to expel him.

Upset, Andy placed an urgent phone call to me and freely admitted, "Pastor Marsha, I messed up."

After telling me his side of the story, I asked, "Okay, what's the procedure?"

"There are three appeals" he explained. "I've been through the first two, and both of them were denied." He continued, "The General I am dealing with told me that in his 30 years at West Point he's never approved an appeal that had already been turned down by the other two courts."

Very dejected, Andy continued, "I'm going to cancel the third one."

"No! Hold on!" I told him. "Let's pray together and stand on the Word. Then go ahead and meet with the General tomorrow and we'll see what God does."

He wasn't too confident, but he agreed. Then I quoted a verse that popped into my mind that very moment: *"The king's heart is in the hand of the Lord, like the rivers of water; He turns it wherever He wishes"* (Proverbs 21:1).

Andy and I started praying these words over the General: "Lord, turn the heart of this man toward Andy with favor." Even after our phone conversation ended, I kept repeating those words way into the night.

The next morning Andy walked into the man's

office and the General was staring right at him, "Sit down, young man," he ordered.

Andy took a seat in front of the officer's desk and the General leaned forward and looked straight into his eyes. "Who *are* you?" the officer asked.

"Sir?" Andy replied, not knowing exactly how to respond.

The General proceeded to tell him, "I have never gone against the other courts in my many years here, but all night my heart was turning. I don't know why, but I'm going to give you a second chance."

When Andy relayed the positive outcome to me, I knew in an instant what had touched the General's heart—the Word!

TIME TO TAKE A STAND!

When it seems that the arrows of the enemy are relentlessly coming against you, don't cower and hide. Regardless of any situation that may arise, exclaim, "Lord, I thank You that no weapon formed against me shall prosper" (see Isaiah 54:17.)

If circumstances look uncertain, pray, "Lord, I thank You that You have wonderful plans concerning me. Plans of good and not of evil. Plans to bless me and not to harm me. To give me hope and a future" (see Jeremiah 29:11).

If sickness arrives on your doorstep, bless His holy name and say, "Lord, I thank You that by Your stripes I am healed and made whole" (see Isaiah 53:5).

As Christ followers, this is how we stand! This is how we live.

I reject the statistic that says 60 percent of children who are raised in church will turn their backs on God in college. Why? Because I stand on the Word that promises, *"Train up a child in the way he should go, and when he is old he will not depart from it"* (Proverbs 22:6).

- Are your children acting like they have no common sense? Start speaking the Word over them.
- Is your marriage hitting a rough patch? Speak the Word over your problems!
- Is your health deteriorating? Speak the Word over your physical body!

Remember, God's holy Word is your faith, your

anointing, your power, and your reality—not your crippling circumstances or stressful situations.

Key #2: Walk in Holiness

Not too long ago it was rather easy to tell the world from the church. Sadly, that line has become blurred. It's not because the world has cleaned up its act, rather it is because the church has become a little muddy. We allow compromise here and there to seep in, and all of a sudden this purifying water isn't so crystal clear. There is no longer the same flow.

We were called to be *"a chosen generation, a royal priesthood, a holy nation, His own special people, that you may proclaim the praises of Him who called you out of darkness into His marvelous light"* (1 Peter 2:9).

As a result we are to look different and act accordingly—not to walk in sin, but in holiness and righteousness.

Many say, "Yes, I understand all that, but we need to relate to the world so people will find it easier to be saved."

I am more than willing to be relative, but not at the cost of compromise. We were called to be set apart—to be separate from the world.

I've heard people comment, "Well, if we're that strict on sin, visitors will feel uncomfortable in church."

If the Spirit of God is at work one of His main tasks is to convict men and women of iniquity—that's what He does.

FACE TO FACE WITH TRUTH

If you think Jesus was easy on sin, look at the rest of the story of the Samaritan woman He met at the well. When the Lord told her about the water that He gives—that is a fountain springing up into everlasting life, she instantly replied, *"Sir, give me this water, that I may not thirst, nor come here to draw"* (John 4:15).

That's when Jesus asked her to go and get her husband and come back to the well. The woman answered, *"I have no husband"* (verse 17).

He responded, *"You have well said, 'I have no husband,' for you have had five husbands, and the one whom you now have is not your husband; in that you spoke truly"* (verses 17-18).

Wow! Jesus didn't sugarcoat her sin, but He called her out—and it transformed her life. Without delay, she became a witness in Samaria. She left her waterpot, ran into the city and announced to the people, *"Come, see a Man who told me all things that I ever did"* (verse 29).

The Bible records that *"many of the Samaritans of that city believed in Him because of the word of that woman"* (verse 39). They testified, *"Now we believe, not because of what you said, for we ourselves have heard Him and we know that this is indeed the Christ, the Savior of the world"* (verse 42).

When this woman came face to face with the truth, it not only transformed her life—but had an eternal impact on many others.

Christ called sin what it was—sin. Yet there are some who say, "I've been saved a long time. I don't drink. I don't smoke. I don't cheat on my spouse." Wonderful, but as long as we are walking on planet earth, none of us can claim to be perfect.

Daily, we need to hold up the mirror of the Word and ask,"Lord, is there anything in me that doesn't reflect You?" Is it gossip? Is it arrogance? Is it pride? Is it selfishness?" Pray, "Lord, examine me because I want to be holy."

You can't have rivers of living water when mud is polluting the stream. It's got to be living, pure, rich water.

God is saying to each of us: *"Blessed is the man who walks not in the counsel of the ungodly, nor stands in the path of sinners, nor sits in the seat of the scornful; but his delight is in the law of the Lord, and in His law he meditates day and night. He shall be like a tree planted by the rivers of water, that brings forth its fruit in its season, whose leaf also shall not wither; and whatever he does shall prosper"* (Psalm 1:1-3).

Key #3: Be Filled With the Holy Spirit

Before we gave our hearts to Christ, the Bible states that we *"were dead in trespasses and sins"* (Ephesians 2:1). We had no life. But now God *"made us alive together with Christ"* (verse 5).

At that moment you started a divine journey with the Holy Spirit. You can hear His voice; you can walk with Him; He can lead you.

It is impossible to recount the number of times the Holy Spirit has protected me—just because I heard Him say, "Don't turn that way." Or, "Walk this path."

On a mission trip to Africa, my companions and I were in a pickup truck in a rural area when we spotted a large, open-back, people-carrying truck on the side of the road. We could see that it was mostly filled with men and it appeared to be broken down. The woman missionary we were with asked, "Do you think we should stop?"

In an instant, the Holy Spirit spoke to my heart, "No." I immediately instructed the driver, "Quick! Turn around!"

"What do you mean?" she asked me.

"Just go," I told her.

The second we turned the vehicle around, about ten men jumped out of the truck and started running toward us, menacingly. It was an ambush—but the Lord wouldn't allow it to happen! We got away without a second to spare because I heard that still, small voice.

The Holy Spirit can not only lead, guide, and fill you, but He is the bearer of awesome gifts. The gifts of the Spirit are meant for every believer.

THE BROOCH

One of the first times I began to hear the voice of God was in Bible School. Most of the students were fresh out of high school, but there was one woman who was in her late 50's or early 60's who had raised her children and felt the Lord calling her into ministry.

One day she came up to me and handed me a piece of jewelry, saying, "This is my favorite brooch, and the Lord impressed upon me to gift this to you."

I really didn't know what to say, because I don't wear brooches—and this one certainly wasn't my style. It was in an old-type Victorian setting adorned with carriages and horses. But the woman insisted: "It breaks my heart to give this to you, but the Lord told me to."

Hearing her sincerity, I replied, "Thank you"—and put it in my drawer.

Five months later, I could hear the Holy Spirit whispering to me, "Take out that piece of jewelry and go find the woman who gave it to you."

I didn't understand, but was obedient.

Just before I handed the brooch back to the original owner, a "word of knowledge"—one of the gifts of the Spirit—came to me. I said to the woman, "The Lord told me to return this to you." She looked perplexed, but I continued, "God would have you know that this is just the beginning of many things He is going to restore to your life. This is just step one."

The woman began to weep uncontrollably. It was

a catalyst, and from that day forward the Lord began to pour out His blessings and return to her things she had lost over the years.

Oh, how amazing it is to be open for the gifts of the Spirit to surge through each of us.

Today, if you feel your waters are murky and muddy, ask God to let His abundance flow once more. No longer will you just be barely breathing—but truly *living!*

CHAPTER 2

DESIGNED FOR DESTINY

For people who don't know God, destiny is often defined as the word, "fate"—meaning that whatever happens or doesn't, everything is meant to be.

In the life of believers, however, destiny denotes something far different. It means the God-given purpose and outcome of life.

One of the most intriguing personalities in the Bible is Joseph. This young man, the eleventh son of Jacob, had God's fingerprint on his life.

Joseph was special to Jacob. Part of the reason being that Rachel was his mother—a woman Jacob loved and worked 14 years to earn her hand in marriage. Just as important, he *"loved Joseph more than all his children, because he was the son of his old age"* (Genesis 37:3).

This tells me that when Jacob looked at Joseph, he saw the future, his legacy, a destiny.

The evidence of what Jacob envisioned was revealed in Joseph's life, who had a divine purpose and the hand of God resting upon him—from his birth until his death.

Without question, this son of Jacob was called for greatness, but as we read the account of his life, it certainly doesn't seem that "great" is the word to always describe his journey. For example, I don't think everyone would say it was wonderful to be thrown into a pit, sold by his brothers into slavery, accused of rape, or to be locked up in prison.

What's truly awesome, however, is that God gave Joseph an incredible dream—which included that one day his brothers would bow before him (Genesis 37:6-7). But from the time he had the dream until it actually came to fruition took more than 20 years.

In the meantime, practically everything he experienced was contrary to what the Lord had shown him. Joseph was walking out what at times seemed horrific, yet God had placed something very different in his heart. Joseph knew this—and believed it with all his being.

Yes, he remembered the dream, but it wasn't tangible. He couldn't see it, touch it, or pursue it. All he could do was to hold on.

The Old Testament is filled with dramatic accounts of people who had amazing God-given destinies:

- Abraham was called to be a father of great nations.
- Moses was called to lead the tribes of Israel out of exile.
- Joshua was called to usher Israel into the Promised Land.

In every case, they lived through incredible hardships and endured difficult places that required courage. You see, the divine never comes unchallenged or is fulfilled without a cost.

A NEW DYNAMIC

Now for the good news. God is still in the business of creating destiny in the lives of His children. For instance, Abraham Lincoln believed it was his God-given mantle to totally abolish slavery. Even today, a not-so-well-known individual named Christine Caine believes it is her calling to help abolish human trafficking in the 21st century.

If you have given your life to the Lord, something special has been planned just for you. Yet there are plenty of Red Seas to part and many mountains to climb.

In the Old Testament, we read of men and women walking arduous paths to reach the place where God is leading them. But in the New Testament a new dynamic is added. Yes, we are moving toward an ordained destination, but God is now forming Christ in us, which literally transforms our journey.

Paul the Apostle paints a wonderful picture of this when he writes, *"My little children, for whom I labor in birth again until Christ is formed in you"* (Galatians 4:19).

It's interesting that this verse would refer to child-bearing. I believe it is because this process is not always a pleasant experience. I've yet to meet a mother who, with delight, said, "Giving birth was a breeze—the best time of my life. I can't wait to do that again!"

They certainly love the child, but wish he or she

arrived in a different way—or that a stork had just dropped the infant off!

God's ultimate purpose is to form Christ in you. He desires to take His hands and shape and fashion you into the image of His Son.

We are headed for a destination, but how we get there and who we are when we arrive is what God is working on at this very moment. As we begin to understand what is taking place, our perspective changes. Now, everything that comes our way has a divine purpose.

In Joseph's life:

- Being thrown in a pit had a purpose.
- Being sold into slavery had a purpose.
- Serving in Potiphar's house had a purpose.
- Prison had a purpose.

If these things had not occurred, Joseph would not have been able to stand in a place of prominence in the palace of the Pharaoh!

THE POTTER AND THE CLAY

It's easy to smile when the seas are smooth and we

are enjoying a good job, wonderful family, etc. But what is it like when you're under the magnifying glass of intense pressure? How do you respond when your integrity is being questioned or you are facing an unexpected trial?

That is when you need to stop and realize that in your darkest hours, if you yield to God's Spirit, He is forming Christ in you.

Can you envision a potter sitting at his wheel with a piece of clay in his hands that is being shaped? This is what the prophet Jeremiah saw when the Lord told him to go to the potter's house. *"There he was, making something at the wheel. And the vessel that he made of clay was marred in the hand of the potter; so he made it again into another vessel"* (Jeremiah 18:3-4). Then the Lord told him, *"Look, as the clay is in the potter's hand, so are you in My hand"* (verse 6).

The potter is God, and the clay represents you and me.

As He fashions and molds us, we are often pressed to our limits—and we may not like the experience. But if God's ultimate purpose is to form Christ in us, we have to yield to His ways. When we do, it doesn't matter where we are in the process, because if our perception is in tune with our heavenly Father, we will look at our problems with new eyes. Instead of wrestling with flesh and blood, we will say, "Lord, what are You trying to teach me? What in me doesn't look like You? What are You changing for my good?"

God may put you "up close and personal" in the presence of an individual who is not loving and tell you, "Love them." He may place you in a situation where your feelings are hurt and your nose is out of joint—not because He is cruel, but because He wants you to mature and grow to be like His Son.

He molds us so that when we are in the midst of a storm, we are not blown away. We hold our ground and stand firm!

IT'S A RELATIONSHIP!

There's a distinct difference between the word "religion" and "relationship." If you simply have religion when you're thrown in the pit, you won't stand, because all religion does is modify your behavior. But if you truly have a living, breathing relationship with the Lord Jesus Christ, whatever the situation, you are transformed.

Paul was in prison when he wrote, *"Where the*

Spirit of the Lord is, there is liberty" (2 Corinthians 3:17). The jail wasn't his final destination, because God was making him a new person.

Your kinship with Christ should always be moving forward. If not, the pressure of wind and water being hurled at you from the enemy and the world is too fierce for you to remain standing. You are regressing, and perhaps don't even realize it.

Learn to press ahead, enjoying a living, breathing relationship with the Lord. Real life is not simply religion, knowledge, or wisdom, but Christ being manifested in your life.

The reason Joseph was able to stand with authority in the palace is because he matured in the pit. As a result, by becoming the man God wanted him to be, he saved his entire nation from starvation (see Genesis 47).

A TEST IN THE KITCHEN

At the age of 19, I enrolled in Zion Bible Institute, in Providence, Rhode Island. It was a new world for me. They had a program where students worked on campus, and my assignment was the kitchen. I was told that the woman in charge was "Sister Doris" from Massachusetts.

The first day on campus, I walked into the college kitchen, smiled and introduced myself. "Hi, Sister Doris, I'm Marsha"—and was about to begin a conversation.

The woman immediately put her hand up and said, "Wait. Stop talking. You're from New York. I know from your accent—and I hate people from New York."

In a brusque manner, she continued, "You guys talk too fast. You think you own the world. You come into every place running your mouth." Hardly missing a beat, I heard, "In my kitchen, from this point forward, you don't speak. You do what I tell you. Don't open your mouth, because I don't want to hear that accent."

Initially, I thought it was a joke and responded, "But Sister Doris..."

She interrupted, "Did you not hear me? No speaking!"

Over the next couple of months, she was just as mean as the first day I met her. Instead of calling me by my name, she would say, "Hey, New York. Can you go over there and get that for me?"

Now I'm a proud New Yorker, but she certainly wasn't saying it because she was proud of me!

One day she grabbed a huge bag of onions and threw it down in front of me. "New York," she said, "I need you to cut all these up."

"No problem," I replied.

For about an hour I sat there slicing and dicing—with onion tears rolling down my cheeks until I could hardly see."

She walked over, examined my work, and yelled, "New York, didn't anybody ever tell you how to cut onions? I can't use these now. I'm just going to freeze them." Then she threw another bag down, saying, "Cut these up"—and told me the exact size of the slices she wanted.

As she was walking away, I thought, "How can I throw an onion at her and still graduate from Bible School and go into the ministry?" Frustrated, I ran out of the kitchen, stormed down the hall, right into the dean's office. We called him "Brother Pat."

While he was still on the phone, I said, "I need to talk to you." He hung up and asked, "What's going on?"

"That woman's not saved," I began.

"What woman?" he inquired.

"The one in the kitchen," I answered.

"You mean Sister Doris?"

"Well, she's no sister of mine," I emphatically told him.

With a big grin on his face, Brother Pat motioned for me to sit down." Then he explained how "that woman" had been strategically placed there on purpose.

When I asked why, he told me, "To get this reaction." He added, "No one has ever stormed into my office before about her, but I'm not moving you to another work assignment until your attitude changes and you start loving her."

Quickly, I responded, "Well, I love her. Can I go?"

"We will see," he replied. "You're going to stay there until you *really* learn to love her. Then we'll talk about it again."

Not a happy camper, I left his office and returned to the kitchen, trying to absorb our conversation and attempting to keep my reactions in check.

A couple of months later, Sister Doris once again yelled at me. This time I reacted by grabbing her in a huge bear hug and kissed her all over her face

—leaving lipstick marks.

"Sister Doris, "I love you," I told her. My words and actions were sincere and honest. God was at work!

The next week the dean transferred me out of the kitchen—and Sister Doris and I became friends.

What was happening? Christ was being formed in me, even though at the time I didn't relish the experience. However, I learned that if Christ is truly in my heart, soul, and mind, I can love *anybody.*

THE PROCESS

Allow me to share three important aspects that will help produce the formation God desires for each of His children:

First, Desire to be More Like Jesus

In the midst of a problem, ask, "Jesus, what would You do? And what do You want me to do?"

Have a heartfelt desire to become a reflection of Christ, even though the process may be painful.

Second: Never Lose Heart

Regardless of what storm is swirling around you,

God is God. He is sovereign, and there is nothing too difficult for Him.

The Lord takes the lessons we learn and brings them back to us at certain times and in different ways. We often make the blanket statement, "I trust God"—and think that covers everything once and for all. Usually, however, this trust comes in layers. The Lord will ask," "Do you trust Me with your finances? Your family? Your home? Your career?"

"THAT TOUCH"

On a mission trip to Mexico, we arrived on a Sunday and I was unexpectedly asked to preach at a church that same night. I hadn't had a chance to open a Bible, let alone prepare a message.

When we reached the small sanctuary, the Lord impressed on me, "I have a prophetic word for this congregation." Instantly I was led to preach on the theme, "That Touch."

I spoke about the woman with the issue of blood (Luke 8:42-48) who reached out and grabbed the hem of Jesus' garment. I explained, "Hundreds of people touched Jesus, but what was different about this woman's touch? It was the touch of faith." Then I added, "I believe this is a prophetic word for you tonight."

I had no idea that the congregation was going through a deep valley. Their pastor, Ricardo, had been in excruciating pain for months and his condition was getting worse.

The members were beginning to lose heart, but that night the church heard this word of faith and took hold of it for their pastor. At the end of the service we gathered around him in fervent prayer and believed God heard our cry.

What I didn't know was that earlier the pastor had gone through a series of tests and they found he had a very large tumor on his back. It had already crushed his pelvis and was still growing.

The doctor sent him home, and confided in certain members of the congregation, "There is nothing I can do for him. In two months you will probably lose your pastor."

That night, as we prayed, the people didn't care what the medical report had been. Deep down, they were believing for a miraculous touch from God.

There is no question in my mind that the Lord

honored the prayers of people who did not lose heart, but truly believed!

Third: Live Every Day of Your Life With Purpose

It is foolish to think that the reason you were placed on this planet is just to get up and go to work every day. God has an ultimate purpose and destiny for you that far exceeds any normal routine.

Think for a moment about Joseph when he was tempted by Potipher's wife. The Bible tells us, *"Joseph was handsome in form and appearance"* (Genesis 39:6). And we know the woman *"cast longing eyes on Joseph, and she said, 'Lie with me'"* (verse 7).

I doubt that Joseph had a special "force field" from God that made him immune to pretty women—and Potiphar's wife was beautiful. Because of her husband's elevated position she had access to the best makeup, perfume, and clothes of the day.

However, because Joseph knew that hour of his life mattered for the Kingdom, and he wanted to be like his Creator, he bluntly said to Potipher's wife, *"How...can I do this great wickedness, and sin against God?"* (verse 9).

His position as a slave didn't matter to him. He

wasn't afraid of any repercussions. Joseph wasn't a slave inside. Joseph was free! And because he honored God—God, in turn, honored him.

Today, have the courage to allow Christ to be formed in you. He will reveal His purpose and lead you into the marvelous, divine destiny He has prepared.

CHAPTER 3

AWAKEN TO LIFE!

As you have probably noticed while reading this book, one of my great joys in life is taking people on missions trips to various corners of the world.

Most days run smoothly, but every once in a while we hit a bump in the road. For instance, I can recall on more than one occasion when a member of our team had too much sun and not enough water—and wound up in the emergency room of a local hospital.

The point being, none of us can live without water. This is true both physically and spiritually.

If we go back to early Bible times, we understand the crisis that was faced when the wells ran dry.

In Genesis 26 we're told the story of Isaac, the son promised to Abraham. But now he is no longer a young boy. He's married to Rebekah and they have twin sons, Esau and Jacob (Jacob became the father of the 12 tribes of Israel).

To say that Isaac was very blessed is an understatement. God had favored him with a tremendous inheritance, including herds and cattle. But as we learn, the day dawned when everything came to a standstill because, *"There was a famine in the land"* (Genesis 26:1). Many of the people headed for Egypt because they heard there were plenty of provisions available there.

However, God spoke directly to Isaac, telling him, *"Do not go down to Egypt; live in the land of which I shall tell you. Dwell in this land, and I will be with you and bless you; for to you and your descendants I give all these lands, and I will perform the oath which I swore to Abraham your father. And I will make your descendants multiply as the stars of heaven; I will give to your descendants all these lands; and in your seed all the nations of the earth shall be blessed"* (verses 2-4).

So instead of moving to the land of the Pharaohs, under God's direction, he left for Gerar, in the territory of the Philistines, where King Abimelek reigned.

Upon his arrival, the local men started asking about his wife. Isaac immediately replied, *"'She is my sister'; for he was afraid to say, 'She is my wife,' because he thought, 'lest the men of the place kill me for Rebekah, because she is beautiful to behold'"* (verse 7).

Some time later, King Abimelek was looking out of his window and saw Isaac and Rebekah having a playful, romantic exchange. He confronted Isaac and charged, *"Quite obviously she is your wife; so how could you say, 'She is my sister'?"* (verse 9).

Isaac confessed that he lied so the men in Gerar wouldn't kill him to get to Rebekah.

So the king issued this decree to the Philistines: *"He who touches this man or his wife shall surely be put to death"* (verse 11).

From that moment forward, God began to bless Isaac tremendously. Scripture records that he *"sowed in that land, and reaped in the same year a hundred-fold"* (verse 12). His possessions became so great that the Philistines grew very envious of him. So much so that they actually clogged all the wells dug by the servants of his father, Abraham. They filled the wells with dirt.

Finally, King Abimelek told Isaac, *"Go away from us, for you are much mightier than we"* (verse 16).

THE ESSENTIAL ELEMENT

Isaac became a pilgrim, looking for a place to live.

It makes sense that if you are searching for somewhere to start over, you need three things: food, shelter, and water.

As uncomfortable as it may be, you can survive without a roof over your head—I've seen this in many parts of our world. And you can exist for a certain period of time without food. Many have fasted 20, 30, even 40 days. But you absolutely cannot live without water. After a few days, your body dehydrates to the point of death. Water is essential to life.

Isaac pitched his tent in a valley of Gerar and had his men start digging up the wells that once belonged to his father—the same ones the Philistines had thrown dirt into. However, when the first well was re-dug, men from the enemy camp came to battle Isaac and reclaimed the well. This didn't happen just once, but four times.

At the fifth well, Isaac and his men dug till they reached water and surprisingly, no one bothered them. *"He called its name Rehoboth, because he said, 'For now the Lord has made room for us, and we shall be fruitful in the land'"* (verse 22).

Isaac understood that the most important thing he needed to survive was to find water—and we can't live without it either.

What About Today?

The water mankind needs now flows from the throne of heaven—from the presence of the Lord and the indwelling of His Holy Spirit.

Years ago I heard this simple phrase and have never forgotten it: "Whatever you feed will grow; whatever you starve will die." This not only refers to our physical bodies, but also to our spirit man.

God continues to speak to my heart that His children need to be fed and nourished with His moving, powerful, living water. It brings an abundant, fulfilling life.

I love the way the prophet Habakkuk phrased it: *"O Lord, I have heard Your speech and was afraid; O Lord, revive Your work in the midst of the years! In the midst of the years make it known"* (Habakkuk 3:2).

He was saying, "I heard about the time Your Spirit was like flowing water; please let this river run again today."

This needs to be our prayer also. You see, we can read what God did in the book of Acts, and what He is doing at this moment around the world, but we

44

need to cry out, "Lord, please let Your water wash over my marriage, my children, and my home, and my life."

Without this outpouring, we become robotic in our actions—just good Christians with few signs of fruitful activity or life.

Please realize that as much as you long to experience God's well bubbling up within you, it is also the desire of His heart. When you join forces with heaven, the result will be so powerful that the thirsty will be drawn to Christ through you. They will say, "Look, there is a refreshing, living spring I can drink from!"

ESSENTIAL STEPS

If your cry is for everlasting water, let me give you some essential steps to help you in your search:

Step Number One: Identify Your Philistine

Each person reading this has something that kicks dirt into the well of their water and causes it to become polluted. It may take the Spirit of the Lord revealing it to you for you to discover its identify.

Today's Philistines look and sound different from those of Isaac's day. Complacency, carelessness, and unforgiveness have become almost normal and natural. When this takes place, our well is clogged and there is no longer life or movement.

Several years ago, when I was a youth pastor, a brother and a sister in our group were tragically killed in a fire. The boy's name was Mina, and his sister, Jenny, was about two years older.

You would hardly know Mina was around. He was quiet and shy, while Jenny was just the opposite. She would enter the room "mouth first," and you'd hear her before seeing her. That was Jenny—gregarious, with an outsized personality.

After moving to a new ministry assignment, I had a chance to reconnect with her and felt it was sovereignly set up by the Lord. We began to text and phone, but when I went to visit her again, I discovered Jenny wasn't the same girl. She was now meek and quiet like her brother had been.

As we started to talk, she began to tell me about issues she was going through in her life and some horrible events that had taken place in her life. I realized that the Philistines had thrown dirt in her well and she no longer carried the joy of the Lord I had once seen so evident in her.

I identified her enemy as unforgiveness and told

her, "Jenny, you have to let go and forgive—there's no getting around it."

"Miss Marsha," she insisted, "You don't know what they did to me!"

"I get it," I responded, "and it was terrible. But you still have to forgive" and I used the example of a huge water supply that had been cut off from its source, and she was the one who was suffering the most.

Her position was entrenched in her spirit: "I can't forgive."

"No," I corrected her, "You *won't* forgive—and there's a huge difference."

You see, life is 10 percent of what happens to us and 90 percent of how we choose to react to it.

"Jenny," I continued, "You have to *choose* to forgive."

We verbally wrestled back and forth and I kept insisting, "If you want life, you have to make the right choice."

A time and place had been set for us to meet again, then I received a text from Jenny: "Miss Marsha, I got in trouble at school today and can't come over. We'll do it next week." Then she added, "By the way, I chose life and have forgiven everything."

That was the day of the tragic fire when she and

her brother went to be with the Lord for eternity.

It is so important that you take the time to identify your Philistine. Whether it is sin, fear, anxiety, laziness, or whatever. Call it out and place it at the foot of the cross.

Step Number Two: Get a Shovel and Begin to Dig!

I often hear people complain, "I don't know what we're going to do with this country. Things are out of control."

As far as I am concerned, dirt has been thrown into the well that is America—and there's no governor, congressman, president, or piece of legislation that can solve the growing problem. The shovel has been placed in the hands of believers.

God is telling His children today: *"If My people who are called by My name will humble themselves, and pray and seek My face, and turn from their wicked ways, then I will hear from heaven, and will forgive their sin and heal their land"* (2 Chronicles 7:14).

The solution is not massive, unruly protests, pickets, or even our voting—the Lord is looking for "My people" to clean out the dirt from our national wells. This is not an option but a command of the Lord.

Some may ask, "How will I know when I hit water?" Believer me, you'll know!

I've seen videos of people in drought-stricken countries digging for water. When they hit the target, no one had to tell them it was time to dance. They splashed the water all over their bodies and began to sing and shout for joy!

The same thing will happen to you, and to our nation, when the debris is cleared and the water is flowing uninhibited once more.

As a country, and as individuals, the answer is the same: *"Repent...and be converted, that your sins may be blotted out, so that times of refreshing may come from the presence of the Lord"* (Acts 3:19).

I pray you will use the shovel God has given!

Step Number Three: Refuse to be Careless Again

Once the water is freely moving, guard the well carefully so that the same "junk" won't clog it up.

I pray that when living water begins to move in our lives it would course into the streets, into our communities, and bring heavenly healing wherever it goes.

The prophet Ezekiel described the vision God gave him of *"water, flowing from under the threshold of the temple"* (Ezekiel 47:1). The water started rising—to his knees, to his waist, and became a river so wide that he had to swim to reach the other side (verses 4-6). It ran into the salt-laden Dead Sea, and all of a sudden everything began to live! (verses 8-9).

Along the banks, trees started sprouting and growing. The Bible says, *"their leaves will not wither, and their fruit will not fail. They will bear fruit every month because their water flows from the sanctuary"* (verse 12).

Recognize that you cannot live without the presence of the Lord. Have the courage to start digging, and awaken to newness of life. It's a river that will never run dry.

CHAPTER 4

ALIGN YOUR LIFE WITH THE SUPERNATURAL

You were not created to live a humdrum, routine, average life. God has a divine purpose and calling that will lift you far above the status quo—far above the natural and into the *supernatural.*

Let me take you back to the time when the people of Israel were living in Egypt under heavy oppression. The Pharaoh in charge at the time was very afraid that the Hebrews would rise up in rebellion against him. So he concocted what he thought was a remedy. It was to have every Jewish male baby killed at birth. He figured: no men, no army, no rebellion!

During this cruel edict, a Hebrew baby named Moses was born. Scripture tells us that at birth he was beautiful and his mother recognized that there was something special about him. Knowing the command of Pharaoh, she hid and protected her son. But it wasn't long until she couldn't keep him in hiding. How can you keep a three-month-old quiet?

She came up with a plan that would make mother's today cringe. She decided to fashion a basket out of bullrushes, daub it with tar, and place Moses inside. Then she *"laid it in the reeds by the river's bank"* (Exodus 2:3).

What faith! When we think about this, it didn't require faith for his mother to make a basket, to walk down to the river, or to even place Moses inside. Faith didn't come into play until she put the basket—and little Moses—into the river and it drifted into the current. That is when it became faith.

That act of total surrender was to be the mantra of Moses' life from that point forward.

God miraculously weaves this baby through the river and brings him into the arms of perhaps the only person who could save his life, Pharaoh's daughter. Upon finding the basket, she figured out it was a Hebrew baby, and eventually decided to raise the child as her own.

A few years later, however, the scene dramatically changed. The Bible tells us, *"Moses, when he became of age, refused to be called the son of Pharaoh's daughter"*(Hebrews 11:24). He could no longer watch the affliction of his people and still live in the comfort and security of the palace. So he left and lived among the Hebrews and suffered with them—even though he could have enjoyed the pleasures of royalty.

One day Moses saw an Egyptian taskmaster beating a Hebrew worker. He became so upset that he *"looked this way and that way, and when he saw no one, he killed the Egyptian and hid him in the sand"* (Exodus 2:12).

The next day, after someone accused Moses of being the murderer, he knew that the king was out to kill him, so he *"fled from the face of Pharaoh and dwelt in the land of Midian"* (verse 15).

HOLY GROUND

Moses started a new life in the desert. As every good story goes, he met a girl in the desert, they fell in love, he married her and started a normal life.

We now find him tending the sheep of his father-in-law, Jethro. Despite his actions in the death of the Egyptian, He loved God and was a man of fine qualities and characteristics.

One day, on the backside of the desert, at Horeb the mount of God, an angel of the Lord appeared to him in a flame of fire from the midst of a bush. When he looked, the bush was burning, but it was not consumed. Moses stopped and said, *"I will now turn aside and see this great sight, why the bush does not burn"* (Exodus 3:3).

Suddenly, God called to him from the midst of the bush: *"'Moses, Moses!' And he said, 'Here I am.' Then He said, 'Do not draw near this place. Take your sandals off your feet, for the place where you stand is holy ground'"* (verses 4-5).

After the Almighty introduced Himself as the God of Abraham, Isaac, and Jacob, He told Moses, *"I have surely seen the oppression of My people who are in Egypt, and have heard their cry because of their taskmasters, for I know their sorrows"* (verse 7).

God's next instruction came as a total surprise to Moses: *"Come now, therefore, and I will send you to Pharaoh that you may bring My people, the children of Israel, out of Egypt"* (verse 10).

Moses questioned, "God, why me?" Moses wanted no part of this. But God assured him, *"I will certainly be with you"* (verse 12).

Once he was confident that the Lord was with him, what Moses really wanted to know was how to answer the children of Israel when they would surely ask, "Who sent you? What is His name?"

God declared to Moses, *"'I AM WHO I AM.' And He said, 'Thus you shall say to the children of Israel, "I AM has sent me to you"* (verse 14).

Moses still wondered, *"'But suppose they will not believe me or listen to my voice; suppose they say, "The Lord has not appeared to you." So the Lord said to him, 'What is that in your hand?' He said, ' A rod.' And He said, 'Cast it on the ground.' So he cast it on the ground, and it became a serpent; and Moses fled from it. Then the Lord said to Moses, 'Reach out your hand and take it by the tail' (and he reached out his hand and caught it, and it became a rod in his hand)"* (Exodus 4:1-4).

OUT OF ALIGNMENT

Moses was never meant to live a normal life. God had a divine purpose and calling over him —just as He has for you and me.

Instead of being ordinary, we are purposed to be

world changers—to rock this planet with the power of Almighty God. The question is, "So why not?"

When God stepped into Moses' life and challenged him with an amazing assignment, a major alignment had to take place.

If you own a car, you know when the front end is off kilter. You lift your hands from the steering wheel and whoa! It pulls to the right or to the left. So you head for a mechanic's garage and he corrects the problem.

I believe that millions of Christians, and the church itself, has moved out of alignment with the supernatural.

PLAN A

On our first trip to Africa, we were in a city in Tanzania called Moshi, conducting a kids crusade; something the missionaries had never done before —and they were nervous. They didn't know if the children would want to attend, or if their parents would even let them.

While we were setting up on a Saturday, a missionary commented to me, "We really need to pray?"

56

"Why is that?" I questioned.

"Because if the power goes off on Saturday, it's not coming back on anytime soon."

We had been there a few days and I noticed that the electric grid shut down every day, but it usually flickered on in an hour or so.

"But not on Saturday," he repeated. "That's when the government offices are closed and there's nobody fighting to put it back on. So you really need to pray."

The announced hour for the crusade arrived and all of a sudden about 300 kids showed up. Even before we started, there were over 500 children who walked in off the streets and packed the building. As we were about to begin, we heard a loud, screeching sound through our equipment and the power died. We all just stood there, looking at each other.

A missionary yelled, "Quick, go get a generator."

As a few helpers stared running, I said, "Everybody stop." They replied, "No, we need to go to Plan B."

I told them, "I understand, but we haven't exhausted Plan A. I need you to pray over this electrical system."

Several on our team went over to an outlet and began to call on God. Suddenly, we heard another charge and everything kicked back on.

Would God have allowed us to run and get a generator? Sure, but He would have watched and said, "I could have made it so much easier for you"—which He did.

God is longing to move with power in our lives and in this world. But we have to reach the place where we align ourselves with the supernatural—to look for it, and press on until it is manifested. This must be our first response, not our second, third, or fourth.

Moses had a divine plan over his life. However, he became out of alignment with God. When the Almighty reached out to him in the desert, He was able put Moses back on course—and the Lord will do the same for you.

How does this happen? Here are three vessels I believe God uses:

First: *God Allows the Supernatural to Flow Through a Clean Vessel*

Moses was an honorable man, but when he came near God, the Lord told him to stop and take off his shoes. Why? Because he was now standing on holy ground.

It is not enough just to say, "I'm a good person and

try to do what is right." To walk in deeper depths with our heavenly Father requires a higher level of holiness.

Never forget that the first part of the Spirit of God's name is *Holy* Spirit. As such, He desires to flow through those who are pursuing a life of purity, where they are cleaning out any iniquity and allowing the reflection of God to be seen in them.

Looking at ourselves in a mirror can be deceiving. We may think we look attractive, but that's superficial. Remember, Moses' mirror was God. This is why he covered his own face in the Lord's presence.

The reflection needed is not ourselves or each other. The mirror necessary for self-cleaning is the Lord. He is the standard by which we measure our lives.

NO SECRET COMPARTMENTS

One of my friends, a married pastor who had been in the ministry for many years, had to give up his church after it was discovered that he'd been having an affair for years. Nobody knew about this failing.

After I finally got over being extremely upset and

disappointed about the situation, I arranged to meet with him and talk it out.

I asked, "How could you preach every Sunday when this was going on? How could you run your church, prepare your sermons, and go out and feed the poor? How could you do this with sin active in your life?"

His answer was simplistic. He told me, "Marsha, it was very easy. I just took that sin and I put it in a compartment. I went about my daily living and did everything else as unto the Lord—everything but this one secret."

As Christ followers, we must realize that we are totally transparent before the Lord. There are no hidden compartments. Since God can cleanse every part of our lives, we must make the decision to let Him—whether it be pride, unforgiveness, lust, or worse.

Yes, there are principles and rules we must live by, but God desires that we are so in love with Jesus that we don't want to hurt or displease Him.

Please take the first step to aligning yourself with the supernatural by becoming a clean and worthy vessel.

Second: God Allows the Supernatural to Flow Through a Humble Vessel

Scripture tells us that, next to Jesus, Moses was the greatest servant who ever lived (Hebrews 3:3).

That is quite an accolade.

The reason for this was humility. As it is written, *"Now the man Moses was very humble, more than all men who were on the face of the earth"* (Numbers 12:3). This is why God could use him.

After Moses yielded to God's direction, his life exploded with miracle after miracle. We marvel at the accounts of the plagues in Egypt, the parting of the Red Sea, and food falling from the heavens.

Can you imagine being hungry in the desert and a chicken falls into your hand? Can you envision being thirsty and water gushes out of a rock?

I once got to swim in the Red Sea. Standing on the bank, I thought to myself, "This water separated and the Israelites walked across on dry ground!" Amazing.

I have an Egyptian heritage, so I made sure I let the Lord know, "I'm on the other team now!"

God used Moses because he recognized that his only confidence was in the "I AM!"

Our education and upbringing are important, but

our courage and assurance are not in these things; they are from the Lord, *"for in Him we live and move and have our being"* (Acts 17:28).

Humility allows us to be aligned with the supernatural. It's not self-deprecating, as if to say, "I am nothing but garbage, so I should be crawling on the floor." Not at all. It is recognizing and being able to say, "God is everything and I am His servant."

Third: God allows the Supernatural to Flow Through an Open Vessel

When God asked Moses, "What is in your hand," he answered, "A rod." Since Moses was a shepherd, that rod (or staff) was a symbol of how he earned his living.

I believe the Lord is asking you and me the same question: "What is in your hand?" In other words, "What are your resources, your talent, your gifting?"

On the same trip to Africa I mentioned earlier we took suitcases filled with socks. Actually, we had collected them for a future trip to Columbia, but so many were donated, I wondered, "What are we going to do with all of these?"

So, at the last minute, the Lord impressed upon me

that we should take as many of them as we could to an orphanage we were to visit in East Africa. We all stuffed socks in every space possible in our luggage.

The Christian orphanage we visited was quite run down, but the kids there were absolutely beautiful —and they really loved Jesus.

The moment we walked in, the children started singing, and their young voices filled the air for hours. What a sight it was to see them with their hands lifted up to the Lord, weeping and worshiping God.

Our team ate with them, shared our hearts, had a great deal of fun, and above all, prayed with them. We even bought the children ice cream.

As we were about to leave, I turned to the woman who was in charge and said, "Ma'am. I feel a little silly. We have come all the way from America and the only gifts I have for you are these"—and I opened a big bag filled with socks.

The director started crying and yelled out, "Children, come. Come and see what these wonderful people have brought us." Many pairs of feet came running in our direction.

She lifted up her head to heaven and exclaimed, "Father, I thank You so much that You heard us pray yesterday when we said, 'Lord, please send us socks!'"

This was a moment of supernatural intervention. It wasn't just socks—it was God!

Let me ask you again, "What is in your hand?"

"DO YOU REMEMBER ME?"

When I was a student at the High School of Performing Arts in Manhattan, one day when I was coming out of the ladies room, I saw a girl sitting in a corner who was obviously high on something.

I was going to walk past her because I wasn't sure what to do, but I felt led to talk to her. So I turned and began speaking to the young lady, who immediately began laughing at me. She slurred out the words, "Honey, you can talk all day. Tomorrow morning I'm not even gonna remember that we met."

I responded, "In Jesus name, you're not only going to remember that we met, you're gonna recall every word I said." I spoke for a moment about how God loved her, and left.

Six months later I saw the same girl. She came running over to me and asked, "Do you remember me?"

"Yes, I do," I told her. "But the real question should be, 'Do you remember *me*?'"

She replied, "How could I forget you. The next Sunday I went to church with my mom for the first time and every word you said came flooding back."

What did I have in my hand? I had my voice—and was open to let God use it. The Lord wants to know, "What can I take from you and use for My glory?"

Moses only had a rod in his hand, but that's all the Almighty needed. In Egypt, when he and Aaron threw the rod down it became a snake—and devoured all the other snakes of Pharaoh's magicians (Exodus 7).

Satan is always ready to attack, but God is able to answer in power and with anointing over your life.

Today, tell the Lord "My heart is clean and my hands are open before You. Use me for Your kingdom."

Align yourself with the Lord and expect the supernatural!

CHAPTER 5

HUNGER—THE KEY TO INCREASE

When Jesus walked the dusty paths of Israel, there were hundreds, even thousands of people who followed Him. Practically everywhere He went there was an entourage—not just the disciples, but others who wanted to hear Him teach or witness the miracles He performed.

But one successful man managed to have a personal audience with Christ, which was no small task. He is known in Scripture as "The rich young ruler."

The gentleman began his conversation by flattering Jesus and asking a question: *"Good Teacher, what good thing shall I do that I may have eternal life?"* (Matthew 19:16).

Jesus answered, *"Why do you call Me good? No*

one is good but One, that is, God. But if you want to enter into life, keep the commandments" (verse 17).

The young ruler wanted to know, "Which ones?"

Jesus began listing them: *"'You shall not murder,' 'You shall not commit adultery,' 'You shall not steal,' 'You shall not bear false witness,' 'Honor your father and your mother,' and, 'You shall love your neighbor as yourself'"* (verses 18-19).

The man told Him, *"All these things I have kept from my youth. What do I still lack?"* (verse 20).

You see, this was a good, religious man. He was moral, spiritually literate, understood the Torah, and knew the rules that he was supposed to keep.

What Jesus said next, stunned him: *"If you want to be perfect, go, sell what you have and give to the poor, and you will have treasure in heaven; and come, follow Me"* (verse 21).

Obviously, this was far too high a price to pay, because when he heard this, the Bible records that *"he went away sorrowful, for he had great possessions"* (verse 22).

Here was a person who went to a lot of trouble to find Jesus and ask Him questions, but when he didn't like the answers, he stood up and walked away.

At first glance, we conclude that the Lord asked the rich young ruler for something he wasn't willing to give, but I feel there is a deeper meaning. It is found in the heart of this man.

I believe he left because he simply wasn't hungry enough.

When we are spiritually ravenous, there is no request too big, no cost too high, or no obstacle too difficult.

THE FEEDING LINES

In America, we have a hard time understanding physical hunger. We see it now and again in certain pockets of our society, but I had never seen the hunger that our team witnessed in Calcutta, India. It has been called, "The poorest city in the world."

In that crowded metropolis, Mercy Ministries, founded by Mark Buntain, feeds nearly 30,000 people every day.

We had the honor of going with them to the feeding lines one morning. We had to be on a bus by 3:30 AM to be out on a field by the fish market, where the fish had been hanging for hours. The stench was unbelievable!

The weather in Calcutta can be unpredictable. On this particular morning, it was rather cool and foggy. The ministry prepares huge tubs of rice that is cooked with nourishing lentils for protein. The daily meal seldom changes.

I can still see the throngs of people coming out of the fog to stand in line. Little children were shivering and the plates in their hands were shaking as they walked up to the feeding line to get their scoop of food. Then they sat on the ground, eating, as the sun rose in the distance.

The rice was piping hot, but the heat didn't bother them. They gobbled it down. If a grain of rice fell on their clothing, they would pick it off and put it in their mouths as fast as they could.

If there were any leftovers and they were offered seconds, the children would run and stand in line again, desperate to fill their empty stomachs.

That morning, nothing else mattered—not the fog, the time of day, or the heat of the rice. No hurdle was too high for them.

The scene will never, ever be erased from my mind.

Nothing Would Stop Her!

This insatiable craving for food parallels spiritual hunger. When I long for God to do something in my life, it is my top priority. I only want one thing—for God to fill that empty space. I am not willing to settle for anything less.

The depth of hunger I am referring to is what we read about in the New Testament when Jesus and His disciples were walking through a region of Tyre and Sidon. A Gentile woman from Canaan sought Him out and began urgently calling, *"Have mercy on me, O Lord, Son of David! My daughter is severely demon-possessed"* (Matthew 15:22). But Jesus didn't answer her; He just kept walking.

The disciples gathered around, trying to hush her. They told the Lord, *"Send her away, for she cries out after us"* (verse 23).

This didn't seem to bother the mother and she continued to loudly yell, "Jesus, Son of David! Heal my child!"

What Christ said next must have sounded confusing to her: *"I was not sent except to the lost sheep of the house of Israel"* (verse 24). In other words, His ministry was focused on the Jews.

Undaunted, the woman began to worship Jesus, again pleading, *"Lord, help me!"* (verse 25).

Once more, Jesus tried to explain to her that He had been sent to the lost sheep of Israel. He told her, *"It is not good to take the children's bread and throw it to the little dogs"* (verse 26).

If anybody had a reason to walk away, it was her. She could have said, "He ignored me. His friends tried to silence me. Now I have been insulted. He just called me a dog! I am out of here!"

However, she didn't care what Jesus called her, all she wanted was for her child to be healed. Not giving up, the woman responded, *"Yes, Lord, yet even the little dogs eat the crumbs which fall from their masters' table"* (verse 27).

She was so hungry for a miracle that even a small crumb would suffice.

At that moment, Jesus turned to her and said, *"O woman, great is your faith! Let it be to you as you desire"* (verse 28). Scripture records that her daughter was healed that very hour.

I believe the Son of God had every intention to perform this miracle, but He was challenging the woman's depth of hunger.

THE TRUE ENEMY

When was the last time you were that famished for God to move in your life? Are you spiritually starved, or just curious and perhaps a little inquisitive? Have you prayed, saying, "Lord, I don't care what the obstacle is, I need You to touch my child, my home, my marriage. God, do a work in me!"

There is an enemy that millions of Christians face—and it is called "average."

Average says, "Whatever I am is just fine. I'm not hungry or full, just average." But this keeps us below what the Lord has for us. This is why we need to cry out to God and tell Him,"I don't want to just scrape through my day, I desire to be radical for You Lord, make every hour count for Your kingdom!"

It is my prayer that you will reach the place where you decide it doesn't matter if you have to get up early, go to bed late, or miss a meal. Your hunger should be to walk closer to Jesus and have God's Spirit fill your empty being.

Your relationship with the Lord will never surpass your hunger for Him. You will grow spiritually as far as your spiritual appetite will take you. God is limitless.

If these words are not resonating with you, perhaps

you need to fall on your knees and confess, "Lord, I'm simply not hungry enough, yet I know I should be. Please increase my appetite so I have a craving for You in me."

The Lord Himself will send His Spirit to satisfy your soul.

"HOW DID IT BEGIN?"

One of the greatest revivals of our generation is called "Brownsville." It began on Father's Day, 1995, at Brownsville Assembly of God church in Pensacola, Florida, and lasted for the next five years.

It is documented that over 2.5 million people attended the nightly services during this outpouring of the Spirit, and more than 200,000 gave their hearts to Christ. There were dramatic manifestations of the Holy Spirit and the flames of this revival spread to congregations across the nation and overseas.

I had the pleasure of spending time with the senior pastor of the church, John Kilpatrick, and asked him, "How did this all start?"

"Sis," he began—that's Southern for "Miss"— "It came out of my prayer time. I was so hungry for God to do something powerful that I would walk the aisles of my church, back and forth, sometimes all night, literally screaming, God there has to be more. It's not possible that this is all You have for Your people!"

Pastor Kilpatrick told me that he was so passionate in his cries out to the Lord that he lost his voice. He did this for months, until God touched a Sunday morning service and sparked the revival that lasted for years.

The Lord responds to hunger in ways that are beyond our comprehension. He will heal bodies, restore marriages, and shower us with favor.

What can take years for you and me to accomplish, God can do in one second at an altar.

Like the woman of Canaan told the Lord, you and I need to plead, "I'm not leaving until You touch me—until You heal my child, until You heal my home, until You heal my future."

When the pangs of hunger begin to awaken you with such an intensity, you become unstoppable in your pursuit of Him.

How do we cultivate this in our lives? Let me share these action steps:

Number One: Learn to Self-Feed
If you are trying to live on only what you are fed in

a Sunday morning service, you're in a lot of trouble.

Think of it this way. The average person consumes at least one or two good meals every day, and your spiritual diet also needs regular nutrition. That's why I am telling you to spiritually "self-feed" during the week.

It's much easier than you think. You can listen to sermons online, study the Bible daily, and read books that build your faith and cause you to grow.

When you were a child, your mother or dad spoon-fed you, but now that you're older, you are responsible for your own dietary needs.

Number Two: Cultivate a Relationship With the Lord

Some try to survive on "Prayer 101"—which is, "Lord, just meet my needs."

Now it's time to graduate to Prayer 102, 103, and 104. These prayers look like this:

- "Jesus, reveal Yourself to me."
- "Lord, speak to me."
- "God, show me Your will."

When you enter into fellowship and communion

with your heavenly Father, you make the exciting discovery that when you speak to the Lord, He speaks back!

I was recently driving through Roselle Park, New Jersey, and pulled over to have some tea at a Dunkin' Donuts. As I walked in, I heard that still small voice of the Lord say, "I have something for you here."

I responded, "Okay, Father."

Once inside, there was a young woman in line in front of me and I instantly knew I was supposed to witness to her.

Looking for a conversation starter, I asked, "What do you like to order here?" But when she ordered tea, I continued, "I like tea, too." I was met with little response.

When she asked for a few packets of Splenda, I chimed in again, "That's like several teaspoons of sugar." She gave a little laugh, but then remained silent.

I was quietly praying "Lord, tell me what to say."

I didn't know how to jump from Splenda to Jesus, but as we were making small talk I glanced at the floor and spotted a Gospel tract. I reached down to grab it, and when I flipped it over, it was stamped, "Evangel

Church"—and I started laughing and she wondered why.

"You know what's so funny?" I told her. "This is from my church."

So I asked, "May I give this to you?"

"Yes. Thank you," she responded.

The Lord whispered, "Pay for her tea." So I told her, "I've got your drink, sweetheart." She smiled and replied, "Wow! This is like a really lucky day for me."

"Will you do me a favor and read this?" I asked her—pointing to the tract.

"Deal," she said, and walked out of the store.

In that encounter, the Lord revealed Himself to me—and to her.

Number Three: Watch for Things that Steal Your Appetite

Have you ever realized how fast your appetite grows?

You just finish a big dinner with your family and sit down to watch TV. Everyone is full, but then a commercial comes on advertising snacks, and all of a sudden someone gets up and heads for the refrigerator. It's like we have a built in automatic response: Snack —Eat!

It must be an animal instinct.

While in Africa, I had a chance to go on a real safari. What an awesome experience!

Early in the morning, our guide drove us to a watering hole in a ravine where hundreds of animals were drinking. He pointed out that this was the highest point of danger for some species because they are so preoccupied with drinking their fill that they could easily be ambushed by a predator. "They're not always watchful and there could be lions lying in wait" he told us.

Immediately, we all started looking around for lions. "I don't see any, I chimed in."

"There are always lions," he said. "They're smart, and lurk about early in the morning."

Then he told us, "When there are lions nearby, the monkeys in the trees will try to warn the other animals?

"Are you serious?" I asked

"Absolutely," he replied.

All of a sudden we heard the sound of monkeys going crazy, and a large group of zebras moved away from the watering hole, turning to each other as if they were having a meeting.

As we looked over to the side, sure enough, there

were two female lions. They had been hiding there, waiting for their moment.

One of the lions tilted her head up and looked at the monkeys as if to say, "One day your not going to be in that tree, pal."

The zebras and other animals have learned the importance of being watchful. If not, they would be breakfast!

OH, TASTE AND SEE!

This was a valuable lesson to me regarding the necessity of being watchful over the things that steal our appetite for God. If we are not careful we can find ourselves in danger.

Right now, I am asking you to pray, "Father, keep my appetite hungering for Your presence." Once you have the Bread of Life, nothing else will satisfy. The world will seem so empty. As the psalmist wrote, *"Oh, taste and see that the Lord is good"* (Psalm 34:8).

May you have a hunger to move above average.

CHAPTER 6

DARE TO DREAM!

One day, Jesus was teaching in a synagogue on the Sabbath when he saw a woman the Bible describes as having *"a spirit of infirmity eighteen years, and was bent over and could in no way raise herself up"* (Luke 13:11).

I want you to picture this person in her stooped condition. Everything about her was crooked and bent over—the way she ate, slept, walked, bathed, and shopped. This was her vantage point.

Who knows who this woman was eighteen years earlier. Whose daughter? Whose mother? What were her dreams and aspirations? But the enemy threw a snare into her life and now her existence was all about brokenness. That's all she knew.

Anyone living with chronic pain will tell you that eventually it becomes part of your everyday life.

By this time, Jesus was well known. So, out of

curiosity, she came to see what was going on. Perhaps she thought she would see a miracle or two. It was exciting, but from her perspective she certainly didn't think it would be life-altering.

This physically challenged woman was not seeking to get the Lord's attention, *"But when Jesus saw her, He called her to Him and said... 'Woman, you are loosed from your infirmity,' And He laid His hands on her, and immediately she was made straight, and glorified God"* (verses 12-13).

THE GREAT TRANSFORMATION

In many ways, we have become like this woman. We are excited to see God move, but we are not necessarily stepping into the fullness of what He has for us. We have no idea that it is *"exceedingly abundantly above all that we ask or think"* (Ephesians 3:20).

From the tiniest baby to a senior saint, God has a divine plan for all of His creation. Yet we will never reach His purpose in our lives without transformation.

Millions have mistaken morality or information for transformation, but they do not produce the change

God desires. The only thing that forms Christ in us is the Holy Spirit. As Paul the Apostle so eloquently wrote, *"But we all, with unveiled faces, beholding as in a mirror the glory of the Lord, are being transformed into the same image from glory to glory, just as by the Spirit of the Lord"* (2 Corinthians 3:18).

God has special dreams and plans for us that we can literally walk in. And when our morality and information are also touched by the Holy Spirit, we become unstopable!

I wish transformation was just a one-shot deal! Wouldn't it be wonderful to be saved today and perfected tomorrow? But the Lord is *continually* changing us. As we yield, we become more like Christ.

The season that lies in our future is far greater than what we have experienced in the past. It is true that the latter rain will exceed the rain that came before (see Joel 2:23), and *"The glory of this latter temple shall be greater than the former"* (Haggai 2:9).

This only happens when our lives line up with the Holy Spirit. He is a gentleman, and does not arrive kicking down doors. Instead, He comes into our presence at our invitation. This is why, as a church and as individuals, we must pray, "Holy Spirit, You are welcome in this place. Move with freedom and with liberty. I am Your child and am open for You to transform me." And that's what happened to this woman. One moment with Jesus and her whole world was revolutionized.

WHAT BRINGS THE CHANGE?

Let me share three "markers" of what transformation looks like:

Transformation Marker #1: You Begin to See With His Eyes

For 18 years, all the "bent over" woman who came to the synagogue could see were feet and dusty roads. But because of the touch of the Great Physician, she was able to stand up and enjoy new horizons.

In our negative circumstances and low vantage point, we often have limited vision. But the eyes of the Spirit are very different; they are full of expectation and hope.

Recently, I was invited to speak at a chapel service for an inner-city Christian school in Brooklyn, New York.

Even though it was founded and operated by believers, the vast majority of the students were unsaved. These kids had lives that no child should experience, and had seen what nobody should see.

They walked into the auditorium, found their seats, folded their arms, and glared at me as if to say, "Okay, who are you and what are you bringing?"

However, I did not allow myself to be swayed by their attitudes. Instead, in my mind's eye I saw heroes of the faith: Deborahs, Ruths, Naomis, Davids, and Solomons.

I began to speak to them about the love of the Lord and I welcomed the Holy Spirit to move in that auditorium. All of a sudden their tense arms relaxed and I started to see tears roll down some of their faces.

At the conclusion of my brief message, I said to the young people, "If you want God to change your life, stand to your feet." All 200 stood up!

I had heard that the street-wise, hardened students had been known not to respond well to a spiritual invitation, but this day the Spirit was at work.

The gentleman who invited me, a good friend, was seated at the piano and had been looking down at the keyboard during this time. When he did glance up, he was so amazed that he actually stopped playing the music! He was completely amazed at the response.

It was a powerful moment because, with God's help, I didn't see the lives these students were living. I envisioned what God wanted to make of them. This is what the eyes of the Spirit can do.

Transformation Marker #2: You Begin to Speak With His Mouth

In the book of Ezekiel we read how God led the prophet into a valley littered with dry, brittle bones —hundreds of them. Then the Lord asked him, *"Can these bones live?"* (Ezekiel 37:3).

The prophet gave one of the smartest answers found in Scripture, because if he said "No," he was going to be challenged. If he said "Yes," the Lord would ask him to make it happen. So Ezekiel threw it back in the Lord's court, saying, *"O Lord God, You know"* (verse 3).

The Lord turned to Ezekiel and told him, "Begin to prophesy over these bones. Command them to come together and they shall live."

Ezekiel describes what happened next: *"As I prophesied, there was a noise, and suddenly a rattling; and the bones came together, bone to bone...and flesh came upon them"* (verses 7-8).

Then God told him to prophesy to the breath—and when he did, *"breath came into them, and they lived, and stood upon their feet, an exceedingly great army"* (verse 10).

It is time for you to start speaking God's Word —that's what prophesying truly is. I am not asking you to deny your circumstances, but speak *through* them.

It's amazing, but when Ezekiel was speaking out loud, there were no listeners. He was talking to bones. You see, the Word of God is so strong and powerful that it doesn't even require an audience!

Transformation Marker #3: You Begin to Live in His Spirit

One of the children's crusades we conducted in Africa was in an area that was more than 90 percent Muslim. Because we posted some advertising, the local pastors became quite worried. They told us, "We're concerned that the Muslim parents know you are here and we don't know how they will react."

In prayer, I sensed a calm wash over me. I felt a caution from the Lord, but not a fear.

Just before the first service, a pastor took me aside and let me know, "It's important that you are finished by 6:00 PM, and not one minute later." He explained, "Our permit says six o'clock, and if you go over that time, they could riot—and we would have a problem."

During the crusade, a pastor told me: "I want you to be led by the Holy Spirit, but if you could avoid saying that Jesus is the Messiah, that would be very helpful." I understood the local sensitivity, and graciously received his advice.

That night, as I began to present a clear Gospel message, I distinctly heard the Lord speak to me, "Don't be afraid. Tell them that I am the Messiah."

I answered "Yes" in my spirit.

I took a few steps forward and boldly declared, "I want you to know that Jesus is the Messiah."

The translator who was standing by my side, turned, looked a me, and asked, "Really?"

"Yes, go ahead," I replied. And so he did. He declared in Swahili that Jesus, the Son of God, was the Messiah.

A row of pastors were seated behind me and I could almost hear the breath exhale from their bodies.

There were Muslim men standing at the back of the auditorium and everyone looked to see their reaction. But they didn't flinch. Nothing happened.

It was almost as if a heavenly army was guarding us.

I continued, "Who wants to know this Messiah?" Practically every child's hand shot up—along with some mothers and a few men.

I would not have been able to speak with such boldness and authority if it had not been for the guidance of the Holy Spirit. In that crusade, more than a thousand children gave their hearts to Christ—most of them Muslims

NO MORE ROADBLOCKS!

After the crusade we were driving down a rough road to another village. In Africa, if rebels or thieves want to ambush a car, they line up rocks in the middle of the road—piled high and thick. There are no streetlights, so you come upon these very quickly.

Several cars were needed for our group. I was in the first vehicle with a team member and a pastor/ translator. Our driver was from a local taxi company.

The Spirit of the Lord weighed heavy on my heart, saying, "I want you to pray right now for protection." Immediately, everyone in our car began to call on God.

While driving in the pitch black, our headlights

shined on a pile of rocks that was almost as high as the car, and as wide as the road!

I could see the cab driver's hand begin to shake because he understood the potential danger. Then the Holy Spirit directed me to say, "Don't slow down. Just drive through it!"

When the translator repeated my words, the driver looked stunned, but he obeyed.

As sure as my name is Marsha Mansour, I am telling you that as soon as we reached the blockade, the rocks fell to both sides and we drove down the middle—just like the parting of the Red Sea! Not one stone touched our car, or the vehicles behind us.

We drove a little further and the road was blocked once more. Again, I told the driver to go right through it. He did, and the same thing happened.

At the third roadblock, he didn't even have to ask. He put his foot on the accelerator, the rocks fell to the sides, and we drove safely through. We finished our journey without harm.

Friend, when God gives you a dream, He will also provide you with power, purpose, and protection. Invite His transformation into your life today.

CHAPTER 7

LIFE ON THE ALTAR

For 40 years, Jeremiah prophesied that if Israel did not repent of their wicked ways and turn back to God, an enemy would appear and take them into captivity.

The nation failed to listen and Babylon conquered the land. The book of Daniel is a recorded account of the events that took place during this time.

The King of Babylon was a ruthless leader named Nebuchadnezzar. He was fearless in battle, but had one fatal flaw—he was extremely arrogant. As a result, he was blinded to many things that were swirling around him.

One day, in his pride, he told the men who worked for him, "Go among the Jews and pick the finest men to work and serve me." The criteria was that they had to be the most handsome, strongest, smartest, sharpest, and most knowledgeable of men.

Many candidates were selected, but only four really stood out as exceptional. Their names were Daniel,

Shadrach, Meshach, and Abednego.

These young men were placed in special training for three years. In order to serve the king, among other things, they had to learn the language of the Babylonians, study literature, history, culture, and eat certain foods.

However, when they saw the king's diet, they knew these foods were an abomination to their faith, so they purposed in their hearts they wouldn't eat them. Yes, they were captives on foreign soil, but they took a stand.

Daniel went to the captain of the army and asked for favor regarding the matter. The captain was scared to honor this request, but the Lord was with them, and and it was granted. They didn't have to eat what everyone else did. God continued to bless them in their new land and they quickly rose in the ranks.

Before long they became personal advisors to the king. Daniel could interpret dreams. Shadrach, Meshach, and Abednego had the gift of administration. With the wisdom God had given them, these men were now sitting at the king's table—advising him, speaking into his ear, giving him wise information, and the king was honoring their counsel.

BEWARE OF THE CRUMBS

Daniel understood a powerful spiritual truth. He knew that any crumb from Nebuchadnezzar's table would defile him. One morsel would lead to another, and before long he would be feasting at the table.

This is how the enemy leads us to fall. He never invites us right up to the table of sin. He throws out one crumb at a time, and with each one we eat, we find ourselves moving from the altar of God to the altar of self and sin.

No one gets up in the morning and announces, "I want to kill myself." Or, "I want to have an affair." These thoughts start one crumb at a time; then one day they suddenly find themselves at the table of Nebuchadnezzar. Those who want to live lives of courage must resist every crumb.

THEY WOULDN'T BOW

I've seen it happen again and again that when God gives favor, secular people usually have two responses. First, they are drawn to them. Second, they become angry, saying, "Why do things always work out for so-and-so?" In Daniel's day it was, "Why is the king listening to these Jews? They don't know anything!"

As Shadrach, Meshach, Abednego, and Daniel continued to be promoted, the king's staff began plotting against them in an attempt to have these Hebrews removed from power.

In the third chapter of Daniel we read the details. Because King Nebuchadnezzar was so great in his own mind, he made an idol to himself, and at the request of his aides, signed a binding decree that when the official music played, every person in the nation, *"shall fall down and worship the gold image that King Nebuchadnezzar has set up; and whoever does not fall down and worship shall be cast immediately into the midst of a burning fiery furnace"* (Daniel 3:5-6).

When the trumpets blasted, the nation obeyed and bowed down, but not Shadrach, Meshach, and Abednego. Immediately, the king's Babylonian assistants ran to him and took great delight in letting him know, "Some of your trusted advisors refused to bow to you." The king demanded, "Bring them to me!"

When Nebuchadnezzar found out who it was, he looked for a way to save these trusted Hebrews, but a decree is a decree. So he offered to give them one more chance to bow when the musicians began playing, then added, *"But if you do not worship, you shall be cast immediately into the midst of a burning fiery furnace. And who is the god who will deliver you from my hands?"* (verse 15).

Boldly, the three remained steadfast in their faith, telling the king they would not bow, and that God would deliver them. Then they added this punchline: *"But if not, let it be known to you, O king, that we do not serve your gods, nor will we worship the gold image which you have set up"* (verse 18).

Nebuchadnezzar simply could not imagine the audacity of these young men, so he commanded the furnace to be made seven times hotter. Then he had the three Hebrews tied and thrown into the fire. The Bible tells us that the flames were so hot that it consumed the men who threw them in (verse 22).

When the king came to look into the furnace, he was astonished, and asked, "Didn't we throw three men into the fire?"

"O king," they replied. "It is true.

"Look!" he answered. *"I see four men loose, walking in the midst of the fire; and they are not hurt, and the form of the fourth is like the Son of God"* (verse 25).

When they were released, *"the hair of their head was not singed nor were their garments affected, and the smell of fire was not on them"* (verse 27).

These young Jewish men had no idea of the outcome of their decision to stand for God, but their commitment was so deep that not even a threat from a king could dissuade them.

THE REMNANT

At the beginning of the story we find that all of God's people were in captivity. How ironic that only three were thrown into the furnace. Daniel himself stood firm for the Almighty. But what happened to the rest of the people of God. They bowed!

Today, it's very easy for us to have the title, "Christian." However, when push comes to shove, "Christian" is not our name—it must be our action, our choice, our lifestyle.

In essence, Shadrach, Meshach, Abednego, and Daniel should be called "a remnant"—and that is what God is calling for in our day and age.

We don't have to look far to see the tentacles of evil reaching out all around us, but the Lord is releasing an anointing over those who choose to be called by His name. Remember, *"When the enemy comes in like a flood, the Spirit of the Lord will lift up a standard against him"* (Isaiah 59:19).

The three Hebrew children did not see the Fourth Man until they went into the fire. They could have talked and debated about their faith all they wanted, but the supernatural did not happen until they were in the midst of the flames. These young men understood what it was to surrender *everything.*

The Lord is calling for people who will not be afraid to say, "God, I'm all about You—without compromise."

Nebuchadnezzar has different names today, but he still exists, and he still demands for us to bend and bow. We must have the faith and courage to say "No" at all costs.

The Bible declares that signs and wonders will follow those who believe (Mark 16:17). The word "follow" indicates that miracles happen when we are in motion—not when we are standing still.

COURAGE TO STAND!

When the turmoil began flaring up not too long ago in Egypt (where I'm from), several bombs were detonated outside of a Christian church in Cairo, killing scores of people who were worshiping inside.

The largest Christian faith sect in Egypt is Coptic Orthodox. It is quite similar to Catholic in doctrine.

Soon after, one of their priests spoke on Egyptian television, which was carried all over the Muslim world. Roughly translated, he said, "Do you think that you scared us? You can burn us, bomb us, stab us, or shoot us, but we are going to serve God. We have a God that is stronger than you and, if He chooses, He will stop your hand. But if not, we are still going to spend eternity with Him."

He added, "We are not going into hiding. We will pray in the streets and in our churches. We will declare Him everywhere we go, because we are not afraid."

When I watched the video of this man, I could see that the anointing on him was overwhelming. Where did this courage come from? I believe it sprang from life on the altar!

LOOK FOR THE SIGNS

Allow me to give you three signs of a remnant people:

Sign #1: Their Singular Goal is to Please the Lord

Scripture tells us, *"The fear of the Lord is the beginning of wisdom"* (Proverbs 9:10). If I'm going to be a remnant people, I will yield my thoughts, my will, and my purpose to my heavenly Father.

Just before the crucifixion, when Jesus was at the Garden of Gethsemane, He knew what lay ahead, yet said, *"Father, if it is Your will, take this cup away from me; nevertheless not My will, but Yours, be done"* (Luke 22:42).

Sign #2: They Are Interested in Doing the "God Thing"

The question we must ask is, "What is acceptable to the Lord and to Him only?"

Are you ready to bend your will in order to conform to His—even if everyone around you is not in agreement? His way is the *only* way.

It's not just the "good thing" we must decide to do, but the "God thing!"

Sign #3: They Daily Live at an Altar of Surrender

I'm sure you remember the day and celebrate the fact that you came to the cross and asked the blood of Jesus to cleanse you from your sins. What a wonderful moment.

In reality, however, we need to fall at an altar of surrender every day we live—from here to eternity. It is all about relinquishing our own plans and yielding to His.

There's a cost involved in being a remnant people. It's our daily laying down of self and turning our lives over to the Lord that breaks the chains and gives us the courage to stand against the enemy.

What are you willing to do?

CHAPTER 8

WHAT HAS STOLEN YOUR SONG?

We often read the word "prophet" in the Bible. It means someone who hears from the Lord and relays what He has said.

There was one man we learn about in Scripture who was so in tune with God, that whatever he prophesied you could totally depend on—his words were as good as gold. That man was Samuel. The Bible reveals, *"The Lord was with him and let none of his words fall to the ground"* (1 Samuel 3:19). As they say today, he was "the real deal"—and Israel knew it.

Samuel was one of the judges God used to rule Israel, to speak over it, give the people instruction, lead them into battle, and correct them. He was God's voice to the nation.

As time went on, however, Israel become like other nations and wanted a king. This broke Samuel's heart, but God told him, *"They have not rejected you, but they have rejected Me, that I should not reign over them"* (1 Samuel 8:7).

Through His servant Samuel, God gave Israel exactly what they asked for—a king. He anointed Saul to that position, and Saul certainly looked the part. Scripture tells us, *"There was not a more handsome person than he among the children of Israel. From his shoulders upward he was taller than any of the people"* (1 Samuel 9:2).

The new king began his reign correctly, being humble, depending on the Lord, and seeking advice from Samuel. But before long he became intoxicated with power. He saw military victories as *his*, and the adulation of the people went to his head.

As a result he began to make ethical compromises —or perhaps we should call it sin. God would give him instructions, which he often failed to fulfill. Then he would blame others for his failures.

One day, God had enough and chose Samuel to tell Saul, *"You have rejected the word of the Lord, and the Lord has rejected you from being king over Israel"* (1 Samuel 15:26).

Saul panicked. He knew that if Samuel was the

messenger, it was the final word from God. Then, as Samuel turned to walk away, *"Saul seized the edge of his robe, and it tore. So Samuel said to him, 'The Lord has torn the kingdom of Israel from you today'"* (verses 27-28).

In the flesh, Saul was still the reigning King of Israel, but the anointing of God over him departed that very hour.

THE LORD SEES YOUR HEART

Then one day, God spoke to Samuel, giving Him this instruction: *"Fill your horn with oil, and go; I am sending you to Jesse the Bethlehemite. For I have provided Myself a king among his sons"* (1 Samuel 16:1).

This was a major occasion, and when Samuel arrived, Jesse brought in his sons, one by one— bragging on each of their abilities. The smartest, the most handsome, etc. The first was rejected, then the second, third, fourth, fifth, sixth, and seventh.

Samuel told Jesse, *"Man looks at the outward appearance, but the Lord looks at the heart"* (verse 7).

Finally, Samuel asked, *"'Are all the young men*

here?' Then he [Jesse] said, 'There remains yet the youngest, and there he is, keeping the sheep"' (verse 11).

Obviously, Jesse thought so little of David, that he failed to present him to Samuel. While he may have been young and insignificant to his father, he was not to God.

The Lord saw David on the backside of the desert, playing music to Him with a heart of worship. When he came into the house, God said, *"'Arise, anoint him; for this is the one!' Then Samuel took the horn of oil and anointed him in the midst of his brothers; and the Spirit of the Lord came upon David from that day forward"* (verses 12-13).

A TURNING POINT

Fast forward to the Philistines waging war with Israel. This is when the giant, Goliath, taunted Saul's army every day. Saul was terrified, not knowing what to do. But this shepherd boy, David, showed up at the camp and pleaded, "King, if you will let me, I will kill him."

I can almost hear Saul chiding him: "You're inexperienced. What do you know about slaying giants?"

Very courageously, David told him, "When I was guarding my sheep, a lion and a bear came, and I had to kill them." Then he made this proclamation, *"This uncircumcised Philistine will be like one of them, seeing he has defied the armies of the living God"* (1 Samuel 17:36).

Saul was impressed with his bravado and allowed him to try. With just one rock from his slingshot, David hit Goliath in the forehead and killed the menacing giant.

When the throngs hailed the shepherd boy as a hero, it set off tremendous tension between the two and Saul turned on David. During the next couple of years Saul tried to kill David at least 22 times. This forced David to become a fugitive and flee for his life. While on the run, however, David formed an army of about 600 men.

While David and his men were out getting supplies, the Amalekites attacked Ziglag, the city they were staying in. They took all the women captive, including David's wives (1 Samuel 30:1-4). Scripture tells us how *"David was greatly distressed, for the people spoke of stoning him"* (verse 6).

What did David do in this dire situation? The Bible records that he *"strengthened himself in the Lord his God"* (verse 6).

David remembered who he was as a shepherd boy and how he worshiped then. It was no different now, so he strengthened himself in the Lord. He regrouped his depleted army, and not only defeated the enemy, but *"rescued all that the Amalekites had carried away"* verse 18)—including his wives.

Victory didn't come when they won the battle, or even when they reclaimed the spoils. It arrived when David strengthened and encouraged himself in the Lord.

This is synonymous with worship. Even when everything seemed lost and his home was burned to ashes, David knew how to sing.

Worship is a creative, spiritual exchange between us and the Lord that opens the door for Him to move on our behalf. When things aren't going well, lifting our hands and hearts to heaven is an act of faith. We can't see God, but we know He is there.

Today, if forces are threatening your very existence and you have lost your song, you can reclaim your voice once more.

David won the battle in his spirit even before he won it in the flesh. It was the same when Samuel anointed him king long before it actually came to pass—which was after Saul was eventually killed in battle (1 Samuel 31).

You see, true courage is worshiping when everything seems to be going wrong. It is one of the greatest catalysts to moving our lives forward in the purposes of God.

WHAT IS WORSHIP?

Here is what we all need to understand:

First: Worship is a Lifestyle

David did not learn how to worship God when his back was against the wall. He was involved in praise to the Lord when he was alone, singing to the sheep, or playing his harp in Saul's palace. Worship was part of his very nature.

For you and me, lifting our voices to heaven should be the daily outflow from a personal relationship we have with our heavenly Father.

Second: Worship is a Spiritual Catalyst

In the midst of heartache, when a child of God starts to worship, things begin to move and shift. For example, before Joshua led the armies of Israel in the battle of Jericho, he *"fell on his face to the earth and worshiped"* (Joshua 5:14).

This was also true when Jehoshaphat was preparing his troops to fight the Ammonites. Scripture reveals how *"he appointed those who should sing to the Lord, and who should praise the beauty of holiness, as they went out before the army"* (2 Chronicles 20:21). Then, *"when they began to sing and praise, the Lord set ambushes against the people of Ammon...and they were defeated"* (verse 22).

Never underestimate the power of an anointed worship team!

Third: Worship is a Choice

I can choose to walk around carrying the spirit of heaviness, or I can shake it off and put on the garment of praise—shouting, singing, and dancing before the Lord. It is my choice.

Since the Lord is worthy of all your praise, make the decision to sing!

HOPE FOR A HEAVY HEART

One of my best friends and her husband were missionaries in East Africa. While there she had a miscarriage, so the next time she became pregnant they returned to the States. They worried that the rough roads in Africa may have contributed to her losing the baby.

Sadly, back home, she miscarried again...and then for the third time. They were both grieving and the husband told his wife, "We just can't do this anymore. My heart is heavy."

None of us are super-heroes—we are all human.

They looked at each other for a minute, not knowing what to do. Then he grabbed his wife by the hand and walked into the living room. He picked up his guitar and began to sing to her. In fact, they both sang a song in Swahili, "Lord, I worship You, Almighty God."

That's all they knew to do to ease their pain. So they stayed there for the next hour, singing, praising, and crying together. Knowing that God was their burden bearer, they lifted their hands before the Lord in wonderful worship. Then he and his wife fell asleep.

Today, their beautiful daughter, Abby, is the love of their life.

Please never let anyone or anything steal your song!

CHAPTER 9

OPEN YOUR EYES!

O ne of the most fascinating characters in the New Testament is John the Baptist. By the description of him, he was rather rough around the edges.

We see him in the desert, *"clothed in camel's hair, with a leather belt around his waist; and his food was locusts and wild honey"* (Matthew 3:4).

Yet John was the one written about by Old Testament prophets. He was *"The voice of one crying in the wilderness: 'Prepare the way of the Lord'"* (Isaiah 40:3). *"Behold, I send My messenger, and he will prepare the way before Me"* (Malachi 3:1).

In the rugged territory of Judea, he yelled out day and night, *"Repent, for the kingdom of God is at hand!"* (Matthew 3:2).

Many recognized that he was a prophet of God, and hundreds come out to ask for forgiveness and be baptized in the River Jordan. This is why he was given the title, John the Baptist.

One day, when he was at the river immersing followers, Jesus came and stood in line. John recognized Him because they were related. Remember, the mothers of John (Elizabeth) and Jesus (Mary) were cousins (Luke 1:36).

When Jesus traveled from Galilee to the Jordan for His baptism, John at first refused, saying, *"I need to be baptized by You, and are You coming to me?"* (Matthew 3:14).

Jesus, however, insisted, and told him, *"Permit it to be so now, for thus it is fitting for us to fulfill all righteousness"* (verse 15). John agreed.

As Jesus rose out of the waters, throngs of people were watching from the river bank. Scripture describes how the "heavens opened," the skies dramatically parted, and *"He saw the Spirit of God descending like a dove and alighting upon Him"* (verse 16).

At that moment, God the Father audibly spoke from His throne in heaven: *"This is My beloved Son, in whom I am well pleased"*

"BEHOLD THE LAMB!"

I can only imagine the charge of divine electricity

that was present on that day.

Immediately after this, Satan took Jesus to the Mount of Temptation where the Lord withstood the devil with the Word of God.

Christ was now ready to launch His earthly ministry. At the same time, John was gathering his own followers, but whenever Jesus came near, John would call out with a loud voice, *"Behold the Lamb of God who takes away the sin of the world!* (John 1:29).

He also bore witness to what took place at the Jordan: *"I saw the Spirit descending from heaven like a dove, and He remained upon Him...He who sent me to baptize with water said to me, 'Upon whom you see the Spirit descending, and remaining on Him, this is He who baptizes with the Holy Spirit.' And I have seen and testified that this is the Son of God"* (John 1:32-34).

John referred to Jesus so often that some of his own followers left him and became disciples of Christ (John 1:36-42).

This did not deter John, who continued to be a prophet in the land, calling men and women to repentance. It wasn't long, however, before John was thrown into prison. Later, we learn why. One day, the

Roman ruler, Herod, was parading by, trying to pass off the woman who was with him as his wife. John, hearing from God, called him out and charged, "That's not your wife. She is your brother's wife. You are an adulterer" (see Matthew 14:1-5).

Herod became angry and had John arrested and imprisoned.

JOHN'S QUESTION

After Jesus chose His 12 disciples and began to minister in the cities, the accounts of the amazing miracles and His teaching reached the ears of John in prison. So John asked two of his own followers to find Jesus and ask Him this question: *"Are You the Coming One, or do we look for another?"* (Matthew 11:3).

Jesus didn't reply with a "Yes" or "No." He simply made this statement: *"Go and tell John the things which you hear and see: The blind see and the lame walk; the lepers are cleansed and the deaf hear; the dead are raised up and the poor have the gospel preached to them. And blessed is he who is not offended because of Me"* (verses 4-6).

In other words, Jesus was sending this message:

113

"John, open your eyes. Look at the fruit of My life."

After John's friends departed, Jesus began to speak to the multitudes concerning John, *"What did you go out into the wilderness to see? A reed shaken by the wind?...a man clothed in soft garments?...a prophet? Yes, I say to you, and more than a prophet. For this is he of whom it is written: 'Behold, I send My messenger before Your face, who will prepare Your way before You"* (verses 7-10).

Jesus lauded the greatness of John the Baptist, but one question remains: How, in a time span of just a couple of months, could John go from seeing the heavens open, the dove descending, saying, "Behold the Lamb of God" and calling Him "the Son of God," to sending people to question, *"Are You the Coming One?"* (Matthew 11:3). What happened to John? What so dramatically changed that John would now doubt what he previously knew to be 100 percent true?

UNDER ASSAULT

Then, Jesus made this incredible statement that almost seems out of place: *"From the days of John the*

Baptist until now the kingdom of Heaven suffers violence, and the violent take it by force" (verse 12).

In truth, however, Jesus was answering John's question. The Lord was saying that the kingdom of heaven had been assaulted. You see, when John was born the enemy not only knew who this "forerunner" was, but that the Messiah was on the way.

For example, the demon-possessed uttered words such as, *"What have we to do with You, Jesus, You Son of God? Have You come here to torment us before the [appointed] time?"* (Matthew 8:29).

The enemy recognized Christ before He ever performed a miracle, and was also familiar with John.

After the birth of John, the devil knew that his own time was short, and Satan began to attack the kingdom of heaven—not passively, not gently, but violently!

In prison, the enemy relentlessly crept into John's mind and thoughts—so much so that his head was spinning and he questioned whether Jesus was the Messiah, and if he should look for another.

Satan's strategy hasn't changed. His desire is to beat you down and so frustrate you that you can't think or see straight. This is when you start murmuring things like, "I don't know if I can make it," or "God, are You really with me?"

He also plants seed of doubt, until you wonder, "Jesus, are You enough, or do I need something else?"

The reason the church is under such incoming fire today is because the devil knows that Christ is preparing His return. He wants you to become so flustered and confused that you won't be ready.

One of the biggest fears of the enemy is that the church of Jesus Christ will actually get its act together and rise to be the dynamic force it is supposed to be. So what does Satan do? He confounds and annoys you until you fail to step out and take a bold stand.

If believers would become the army God has called us to be, the fruit of our lives would be demonstrated as it was in Jesus's life. We would declare, "The blind see, the deaf hear, the lame walk, the dead are raised!" Hallelujah!

I'VE MADE MY CHOICE!

When I was young girl, I believed every word I read in Scripture. I would tell pastors about what I expected to see in every service. And often the response was, "Oh, honey, isn't that sweet."

May I let you in on a secret. I'm still that little girl

who takes hold of the Word of God and says, "Are you sick? Let's pray." Almighty God can heal lupus, fibromyalgia, cancer—and a thousand other diseases.

- Either God's Word is everything, or it is nothing!
- Either I believe it in totality or I throw the whole thing out.
- Either it is my standard for living, or it's not.

Thank God, I've opened my eyes and have made my choice!

FAITH BUILDING STRATEGIES

I constantly run into men, women, and young people who are being beaten down from every direction. They lose heart and lose faith, praying just to make it through the day instead of realizing we should be conquering giants. We must believe God for the mighty, not the mediocre

When you begin to flex your spiritual muscles and stretch your faith, it may seem like all Hell is coming at you—and it is.

Let me share three faith-building strategies that will make a day and night difference in you spiritual walk:

First: Live in God's Word

When Jesus had fasted for 40 days on the Mount of Temptation, He was hungry, so Satan tried to coerce Him to turn stones into bread. How did Jesus respond? *"It is written, 'Man shall not live by bread alone, but by every word that proceeds from the mouth of God'"* (Matthew 4:4).

With every temptation, Jesus did not debate the devil with His own words, but with the Word of God. He continued to repeat the words, "It is written! It is written!"

As believers, we need to *live* in the Word—not just read it now and again when we have nothing better to do. Day and night, it should be our spiritual food.

Let me recommend that you read the Scriptures out loud, because *"faith comes by hearing, and hearing by the word of God"* (Romans 10:17).

Second: Live in God's Presence

I've found that it is impossible for Satan to tie me down when I make the decision to move into the presence of the Lord. This is true because when we are *in* Christ and *with* Christ, liberty is an automatic byproduct.

Jesus stated emphatically: *"Whom the Son sets free is free indeed"* (John 8:36). The chains of the enemy will bind you no longer.

Third: Trust God's Character

Jesus is telling each of us, "Open your eyes. You may not have understood some of the things I've done, but I have worked everything for your good. I have touched your body, sustained you, saved you from your own foolishness, and rescued you time and time again."

He is reminding us, *"Trust me. I am always faithful, have your best in mind, and will always bring victory."*

GOD HAS YOUR BACK!

The enemy knows when we are at our most vulnerable; that is when he attacks. As Eve found out, Satan isn't dumb—he is as smart as a serpent!

It's sometimes difficult to remember God when you are in a dark cold place, afraid. There's trouble brewing at home, at work, at school—and your back is up against the wall. But this is not the time to cave.

When Satan doubles his fist and punches you —punch him back! Be bold, tenacious, and tell him, "God is on my side, and I'm barreling through!"

Claim the fact that the victory is already yours, because at the end of the day, this bully has already lost the battle. He knows his time is short and Jesus is about to return as He promised.

Today, open your eyes and see the glory of the Lord!

CHAPTER 10

SPIRIT REFLECTED, SPIRIT EMPOWERED

In many ways, the book of Psalms reads like an autobiography of the life of David. He was writing them as a shepherd boy, when fighting his enemies, hiding in caves, and after he was anointed king.

However, when God gave David everything He promised—wealth, success, and the royal throne—we don't find him writing the volume of psalms as he did before. Perhaps he was relaxing, enjoying the "good life."

David had some horrendous personal failures in his life, which eventually led him to cry out to God, *"Wash me thoroughly from my iniquity, and cleanse me from my sin...Purge me with hyssop, and I shall be clean; Wash me, and I shall be whiter than snow"* (Psalm 51: 2,7).

Let's examine what brought him to that place.

Most people point to David's sin with Bathsheba as the start of his downward spiral, but something took place *before* that.

The first verse of 2 Samuel 11 tells us, *"It happened in the spring of the year, at the time when kings go out to battle, that David sent Joab and his servants with him, and all Israel; and they destroyed the people of Ammon and besieged Rabbah. But David remained at Jerusalem."*

Joab was just the captain of the army, not the king God appointed to lead the troops. So David wasn't where he was supposed to be. It's been said, "If you aren't in the right place, you're in the wrong place." It was true then, and is still true today.

If David had been faithful to his own responsibility, he would have been leading the battle against the Ammonites. Instead, because he was derelict in his duties, he stayed behind—which led to his second transgression.

IN PANIC MODE!

One day, while walking on the flat top of his palace, he looked across to another rooftop and saw a woman bathing. He was struck by her beauty, and instructed his men, "Find out who she is."

They returned, telling him, "That's Bathsheba, the wife of Uriah, who is a soldier fighting in your army."

After learning she was married, and that her husband was with the troops, he asked his associates to bring the woman to him. David slept with her, then sent her back home.

A couple of weeks later, Bathsheba sent him this message: "David, I'm pregnant."

As you can imagine, he went into panic mode, thinking, "How do I fix this? What can I do?"

Then he had an idea. David had a note carried to Joab, which read, *"Send me Uriah the Hittite"* (2 Samuel 11:6)

When the soldier stood before the king, David commented, "I'm curious. How is the battle going?"

After Uriah gave him a first-hand report, David, said,"Let me personally thank you. Why don't you take some time off and go home to your wife for the night—then return to the conflict later." David hoped that Uriah would sleep with Bathsheba, believing he would impregnate her and his sin would be covered up.

What a shock when David learned that Uriah never

entered the house—he slept outside. David urgently called for him, asking, "Why didn't you go inside your home?"

His answer was surprising: *"The ark and Israel and Judah are dwelling in tents, and my lord Joab and the servants of my lord are encamped in the open fields. Shall I then go to my house to eat and drink, and to lie with my wife? As you live, and as your soul lives, I will not do this thing"* (verse 11).

David realized this was going to be much more difficult than he thought. So the next day he fed Uriah, got him drunk with wine, and sent him home again. But true to his word, the soldier slept outside of his marital home.

Time for another plan! King David wrote a letter to Joab: *"Set Uriah in the forefront of the hottest battle, and retreat from him, that he may be struck down and die"* (verse 15).

He handed the sealed letter to Uriah with the order: "Take this to Joab and give it to him personally. Do not open this under any circumstances."

Joab did exactly what his king commanded and, as planned, Uriah died in battle and was buried. He had delivered his own death sentence!

As far as David was concerned, Uriah was not the

only thing that was buried. He had buried all his sins, mistakes, and treachery. They were hidden in a deep compartment of his heart where he thought no one would ever know about them.

David married Bathsheba; they had a son, and life went on as if none of this had ever happened.

A MOMENT OF TRUTH

Three years later, the prophet Nathan showed up at David's door and asked, "May I talk with you?"

Politely, David, welcomed Nathan into the palace. The prophet told the king, "I need you to rule on a certain matter."

"I'm listening," David replied. "What would you like me to judge?"

Nathan began: *"There were two men in one city, one rich and the other poor. The rich man had exceedingly many flocks and herds. But the poor man had nothing, except one little ewe lamb which he had bought and nourished; and it grew up together with him and with his children. It ate of his own food and drank from his own cup and lay in his bosom; and it was like a daughter to him"* (2 Samuel 12:1-3).

Nathan continued, *"And a traveler came to the rich*

man, who refused to take from his own flock and from his own herd to prepare one for the wayfaring man who had come to him; but he took the poor man's lamb and prepared it for the man who had come to him" (verse 4).

When David heard the story, he became enraged and said to the prophet, *"As the Lord lives, the man who has done this shall surely die! And he shall restore fourfold for the lamb, because he did this thing and because he had no pity"* (verses 5-6).

Nathan looked straight into the eyes of David and told him, *"You are the man!"* (verse 7).

The prophet reminded David that God had delivered him from the hand of Saul and anointed him as king over Israel—and would have given him more. Then he asked, *"Why have you despised the commandment of the Lord, to do evil in His sight? You have killed Uriah the Hittite with the sword; you have taken his wife to be your wife"* verses 9)—and he pronounced God's wrath on David.

King David quickly fell to his knees in repentance, saying, *"I have sinned against the Lord"* (verse 13).

Nathan comforted him: *"Today the Lord has put away your sin; you shall not die"* (verse 13).

THE CAUSE OF FAILURE

It is an incredible story. As you follow the time line, it's almost overwhelming to see how far David progressed from being a shepherd boy in the fields of his father—from one who wrote beautiful songs and loved God to a person who would commit the atrocities of deceit, adultery, murder, and manipulation.

To find the cause of his failure, we need to go back and take a look at who David was as a young man. As a shepherd, he had a lifestyle of quietness. This is why he could write, *"Meditate within your heart...and be still"* (Psalm 4:4) and *"He makes me to lie down in green pastures; He leads me beside the still waters"* (Psalm 23:2).

But as his life progressed to a place of power, he moved away from his closeness with the Lord. If he had stayed immersed in God's presence, he would have been convicted of his sins.

An essential component of stillness is reflection. I am not speaking of self-reflection (which can be beneficial at times), but Spirit-reflection.

Examining one's self has a tendency to be biased—we either see ourselves as too good or too bad. But Spirit reflection is a much deeper insight. It is where we allow the Holy Spirit to speak to us; to hold up a mirror and show us the truth.

In the secular media, I've heard the phrase, "Everyone has to live their truth." This is polar opposite from the fact that there is only *one* truth. Jesus said, *"I am the way, the truth, and the life"* (John 14:6).

In a season of stillness, we allow the Holy Spirit to speak to us; to instruct us in living humbly and righteously. One of His tasks is to remove what is not of Christ. He is the only true reflection of our lives.

CONVICTION! CORRECTION!

David was able to live for three years with sin in his life because he had put all of his iniquities into a compartment.

Today, we can determine how close we are to someone by how we act when we invite them to our home. On the first visit we may just let them see the living and dining room and the guest bathroom. We don't want them roaming freely all over the house because some of the bedrooms might not be neat and tidy. However, when they have been friends for years, we no longer worry where they go—what they see is what they get!

This is a simple example of not permitting God into certain hidden compartments of our lives, because they are "messy." But we must allow His Spirit to search every room.

I doubt that the Lord's first attempt to grab David's attention was to send the prophet Nathan. I believe He had been knocking on the door of David's heart the entire time.

Finally, God's Spirit was able to convict and correct David—to speak into his life. From that point on, we begin to read new psalms where he is pouring out his heart to the Lord once more.

A NEW LIFESTYLE

It was only after God sent the prophet Nathan to confront David, which resulted in repentance, that he was able to write Psalm 51: *"Wash me, and I shall be whiter than snow...Create in me a clean heart, O God, and renew a steadfast spirit within me. Do not cast me away from Your presence, and do not take Your Holy Spirit from me. Restore to me the joy of Your salvation"* (verses 7,10-12).

One of the most powerful prayers David ever uttered was when he asked God, "Do not take Your Holy Spirit from me."

He saw what happened to King Saul—and was an eyewitness to Saul's demise. So he certainly didn't want that to be his legacy—nor does it have to be ours. Each one of us can be a candidate for the Sprit-reflected life.

It is not too late. Starting now, you can take the necessary steps to avoid the pitfalls that caused David so much heartache.

Here is what I recommend:

Cultivate a Lifestyle of Stillness

When it is just the Lord and you, He is able to seize your attention. This is why we need shut off the television, click off the iPad, silence our cell phone, and give God our total focus.

He is saying to you right now, *"Be still and know that I am God"* (Psalm 40:10).

Cultivate a Lifestyle of Spirit-Reflection

The only time you can see a reflection is when the water is still. As believers, we can stay where we are or we can find a quiet place to allow the Spirit to show us ourselves—to probe deeper and peel away the layers of who we are.

Remember, *"But we all, with unveiled face, beholding as in a mirror the glory of the Lord, are being transformed into the same image from glory to glory, just as by the Spirit of the Lord"* (2 Corinthians 3:18).

Cultivate a Lifestyle of Spirit-Empowerment

Only when we pause in God's presence and reflect on His Spirit do we make room for the Lord to empower us. Jesus made this promise: *"You shall receive power when the Holy Spirit has come upon you"* (Acts 1:8).

We spend too much time trying to figure out how to overcome sin, but the answer to iniquity is a Spirit filled life. As Scripture so clearly states: *"Walk in the Spirit, and you shall not fulfill the lust of the flesh"* (Galatians 5:15).

The life we are talking about begins on our knees—when we have the courage to pray, "Lord, remove anything within me that is not of You. Take my heart of stone and give me a heart of flesh that is able to move and grow as You desire.

That's what it takes to live the Spirit-reflected, Spirit-Empowered life.

CHAPTER 11

THE COURAGEOUS WORSHIPER

I have had the pleasure of leading three missions trips to Guadalajara, Mexico—all to the same location and working with the same missionaries.

On more than one occasion, I've been asked, "What's the difference in each trip?"

At the time of these journeys I wasn't able to have an overview of what God was doing but, in retrospect, I now see a clear pattern. Each trip had a unique purpose.

Team #1 Planted Seeds

On our first effort, we dug fresh ground, literally! It was a new field for us and we planted seeds and established relationships with the churches, with the children, and with the missionaries.

Team #2 Watered the Seed

During our second journey, we had numerous problems trying to reach our destination. Our flight was cancelled, we had trouble rebooking seats for everyone—and on and on.

I firmly believe the enemy was thinking, "If I let them go back and care for what they have sown, they will return again and reap a harvest."

God was faithful, and we watered old relationships, nurtured what had been planted, and saw new growth.

Team #3 Reaped a Harvest

On our third mission, the moment we arrived in beautiful Guadalajara, the Lord gave us this word: "Don't say the harvest is in three months, or in nine months. The reaping begins today!"

What a joy to report that we saw miracle after miracle in hungry hearts and empty lives.

Looking at the big picture, if the first and second teams had not forged the way with their hard work and prayer, there would not have been anything to harvest. It let us know that God works in seasons, fulfilling His divine purpose.

THE JOURNEY

In this fast-paced, drive-thru, give-it-to-me-now world, we also want instant answers from heaven. But God sets His own timetable. He sees our hearts and responds accordingly.

Let me tell you about one journey that should have taken only 11 days, yet ended up taking 40 years to complete!

Before God sent Moses to free the Israelites from Egypt's bondage, they and their ancestors had been enslaved by the Pharaohs for more than 400 years.

Finally, through a series of miracles, they were set free and began their amazing journey to the Promised Land—*"a land flowing with milk and honey"* (Exodus 3:8). Even more, it would be a place of freedom and liberty.

As the Hebrews left Egypt, we read the accounts of some of the most amazing miracles ever recorded:

• The Red Sea parted, allowing the Israelites to escape from the chasing Egyptian army (Exodus 14:22).

- Pharaoh's forces were destroyed in the Red Sea (verses 23- 30).
- Marah's bitter waters were made sweet (Exodus 15:25).
- Manna was sent from heaven (Exodus 16:4-31).
- A large flock of quails landed in the Israelite camp in order to provide them with meat (verse 13).
- Moses struck a rock in Horeb and it produced water (Exodus 17:5-7).

THE DANGER OF DISBELIEF

I've met many who have the time line of Israel's wanderings all mixed up. They think Moses and the Hebrews spent 40 years in parched desert before coming close enough to the Promised Land to send out the 12 spies to give them a report of Canaan.

This is incorrect. The spies were sent much earlier, and they spent 40 days secretly checking out the land God told them would become their home.

Here was the problem. Of the spies (chosen from each of the 12 tribes of Israel), only two, Joshua and

Caleb, returned with a glowing, optimistic report. They informed Moses and the assembled throng that the land *"truly flows with milk and honey, and this is its fruit"* (Numbers 13:27)—holding up pomegranates, figs, and huge clusters of grapes. Yes, they saw tall, strong men there, but pleaded, *"Let us go up at once and take possession, for we are well able to overcome it"* (verse 30).

The ten other spies, however, had a different perspective. They talked of *"a land that devours its inhabitants, and all the people whom we saw in it are men of great stature. There we saw the giants...and we were like grasshoppers in our own sight, and so we were in their sight"* (verse 32).

Who did the children of Israel choose to believe? You guessed it—the naysayers!

Their attitude set off a rebellion against Moses and Aaron. The whole congregation cried out, *"If only we had died in the land of Egypt! Or if only we had died in this wilderness! Why has the Lord brought us to this land to fall by the sword, that our wives and children should become victims? Would it not be better for us to return to Egypt?"* (Numbers 14:2-3).

They talked among themselves about selecting a

leader and returning to the land of Pharaoh—and, in their anger, were ready to stone Joshua and Caleb.

God spoke to Moses, asking, *"How long will these people reject Me? And how long will they not believe Me, with all the signs which I have performed among them? I will strike them with the pestilence and disinherit them, and I will make of you a nation greater and mightier than they"* (verses 11-12).

Moses pleaded with the Lord to pardon the rebellious, but God told him that only Josuha and Caleb, and those under their leadership, would see the Promised Land. As for the rest, the Almighty declared, *"Your sons shall be shepherds in the wilderness forty years, and bear the brunt of your infidelity, until your carcasses are consumed in the wilderness. According to the number of the days in which you spied out the land, forty days, for each day you shall bear your guilt one year, namely forty years, and you shall know My rejection* (verses 33-34).

This was the *start* of the 40-year wilderness journey. The reason that the vast majority never saw Canaan is because they had only *physically* left Egypt. Their hearts, their spirits, and everything else about them had remained behind.

Think how close they were to tasting the delights of milk and honey! But they wouldn't move forward because they had lost their courage. They were scared and had no fight in them. As a result they trekked around in circles until they died!

They saw themselves as grasshoppers, and so they became. Numbers 13:32 could have just as easily read, "They saw themselves as *lions*, and so they became." Unfortunately, they chose the grasshoppers!

TAKE THE FIRST STEP

Thank God, a new generation with a new spirit rose up—ready to reap the harvest of everything God had promised.

When Moses drew his last breath, God appointed Joshua as the new leader—and Caleb was right by his side. I can almost hear Joshua saying, "My sword was ready 40 years ago. Can we now go and fight?"

As they approached the Jordan River, the Great Jehovah told Joshua, *"Arise, go over this Jordan, you and all this people, to the land which I am giving to them—the children of Israel. Every place that the sole of your foot will tread upon I have given you, as I said to Moses"* (Joshua 1:2-3).

Then God said, *"Be strong and of good courage, for to this people you shall divide as an inheritance the land which I swore to their fathers to give them. Only be strong and very courageous, that you may observe to do according to all the law which Moses My servant commanded you; do not turn from it to the right hand or to the left, that you may prosper wherever you go"* (verses 6-7).

God didn't tell Joshua, "Be strong and of good courage" just once. He didn't even say it twice, but *five* times (Joshua 1:1,7,9,18, and 25).

- When God says something once, He means business.
- When God speaks twice, write it down.
- When God repeats it five times, you'd better chisel it on your heart!

As they came near the water's edge, God instructed Joshua to line up the people by tribes, and let the Levites (the priests) carry the Ark of the Covenant —and when they step off of the bank, *"the waters of the Jordan shall be cut off, the waters that come down from upstream, and they shall stand as a heap"* (Joshua 3:13).

This was a contrast from what took place at the Red Sea, where the people saw the miracle coming. Moses lifted up his rod, the waters parted and they walked across on dry ground.

Now, God turned the tables. He told them, "I am not parting the waters until you take the first step and walk into the river. And they did.

God made it very clear to Joshua: "If you will do your part—by being strong and courageous—I will do Mine. I will never leave you, nor forsake you. And you will never have to walk alone."

From the battle of Jericho to taking total possession of the Promised Land, Joshua was not only brave and fearless. he never stopped worshiping the true and living God.

WORSHIP WITH COURAGE

Before we ever left on the mission trips to Guadalajara mentioned earlier, the Holy Spirit said to me, "I am going to give you every place that you put your foot in that city—and you will see a great victory."

God is faithful. His promise became a reality. We prayed with scores of men, women, and young people who give their lives to Christ. Sick bodies were healed, and even people with severe depression, on the brink of suicide, were miraculously delivered!

On the first Monday morning, when we started our Vacation Bible School, we knew the Lord was about to do something that was far beyond our own abilities. You see, God always equips, and then He sends.

That's what He did with Joshua, telling him, *"Be strong and of good courage"* (Joshua 1:9)—as he led the children of Israel across the Jordan into Canaan, because, *"Every place the sole of your foot will tread upon I have given you"* (verse 3).

In Guadalajara that day, He prepared us; He filled us. We could not stop singing, laughing, or rejoicing; we were overwhelmed with the presence of God.

Our VBS was in a place called Coli, one of the poorest areas of the city. It has conditions that no child should live in. After one of our team members had to go to one of the houses to use the bathroom, she came back visibly shaken by what she saw. It was a tiny, makeshift hovel that was home to 12 people—with crawling bugs and poverty you can't imagine.

These were the children we had come to minister to—and it was certainly a challenge. There were very few fathers around, so the boys were unruly. My job was to keep them from making a mess, stealing our snacks and supplies, setting fire to the garbage, lying, or bullying the other kids for their stuff. So I placed myself on "bully patrol" while the rest of our team was conducting VBS.

We started on Monday with about 200 kids, but by Thursday the number had grown to over 400—which was a real test for our 17-person team.

Thankfully, the grace of God rested over our VBS in a miraculous way. One of the missionaries kept saying, "I've never seen it so calm around here."

We poured our lives and our love into these children and the Lord met us every day. We rested on His promise, "Be strong and of good courage and I'll take care of everything else."

During this awesome ministry, we seized every possibility, grabbed every opportunity, and God faithfully showed up each time.

NOT ENOUGH BOXES?

I'll never forget "snack time." There were young boys lying and manipulating our team members, trying to get double or triple snacks. One youngster said, "Momma, I'm so hungry. I haven't eaten all day"—but he had crumbs all over his lips from what he had stolen from other kids.

On the final day there was a local woman who had been coming to help us. She was not a believer, but was a friend of the missionaries and seemed to enjoy being around them. She wasn't sure why, but now we know.

She came up to me and said, "Pastor, you've got a big problem."

"What do you mean?" I wanted to know.

"Well," she continued, "You have 320 boxes of snacks and you have over 400 children."

"Are you sure?" I asked her.

She answered, "I've counted them eight times and there are only 320 boxes."

So I decided to count them myself and she was absolutely right, we didn't have enough. So I asked her, "Are there any more left in the vans?"

She said, "I've already checked. There's nothing there."

I looked around and there wasn't anyone free to run to the store and get the huge number of extra snacks we needed—nothing like a Costco in that run-down area. So I rushed down the block to a *bodega* (Spanish for a mini-mart), thinking I could buy something, but they only had five bags of chips.

When I returned and began looking around, trying to figure out what to do, finally, me and several members of our team walked over to the snacks and we were about to pray over them.

The friend of the missionary was watching us and she came over to ask, "Excuse me. What are you doing?"

I quickly responded, "We're going to pray over these."

Puzzled, she said, "What?"

I repeated, "We're going to pray over the snacks."

"Why?" she wanted to know.

"So that God will bless them and multiply them so we will have enough for everybody."

She looked at me as though I had lost my mind,

and told me one more time: "You have 320 snacks, and you have over 400 children. You don't have enough."

"I understand," I calmly replied.

Still not satisfied, the women continued, "I have counted them eight...." I interrupted, "I got it. You counted them eight times, and I counted two more, so that makes ten times. You're right. There's not enough. That's why we are going to pray over these snacks because I believe God will bless them."

The local woman walked away and began to complain to Julie, another member of our team, telling her what was going on—"And Marsha is praying up there."

Julie said, "That's a great idea," and came over to pray with us.

We divided the kids into four groups of 100, and started handing out the snack boxes. And when we got to the last group which was about 120, I said to the doubting volunteer, "Come over and help us."

When kid number 320 came by, there were still more snack boxes. Then 340, 380, 400, 420—and there was one box left over. I felt it was God's little signature at the end!

The woman was dumbfounded. "What just happened?" she asked.

"God just blessed and multiplied the snacks!" I told her. "Yeah, God is so cool that He left a box for you to take home to your family."

She didn't know how to react, and I watched as she sat on a bench for a couple of minutes, completely undone by what she had witnessed with her own eyes!

POSSESS THE LAND!

God is so good. He is willing to show up and do the miraculous in your life. You have a God who is limitless, who can do great and mighty things. He is saying, "Put your foot in the water and I will part it." But remember, you have to take the first step.

None of us are on a mission that only lasts for 10 days; we should all be on a mission for Christ every day of our lives.

Remember, the Lord equips us, then He sends us. He prepared Joshua by speaking into his very soul: "Be strong, and of good courage. Now go!"

From your heart, lift up your voice and sing:

We are able to go up
*   and take the country,*
And possess the land,
*   from Jordan to the sea.*
Though the giants may be there
*   our way to hinder,*
Our God has given us the victory!

CHAPTER 12

ALIVE, ALERT, AND OVERFLOWING!

T he book of Matthew is written to a very specific audience—the Jews. On its pages you will find constant references to Old Testament prophecy.

Jesus was led to say certain things to fulfill the prophecies of Daniel, Jeremiah, and Ezekiel. He was convincing the Jews that He was the Messiah they had been waiting for.

Matthew's writings are very intricate, detailed, and parallel the Old Covenant. He speaks more about the Pharisees and Sadducees than any other writer of Scripture, because he is attempting to show the Jewish religious leaders of the day that Jesus is the one for whom they had been searching.

The Jews did not understand that there were *two* comings of the Messiah. This is why Matthew has more teaching in his book concerning the second coming of Christ, the end times, and the Tribulation, than other writers.

149

THE WISE AND THE FOOLISH

In this gospel, Jesus gives us a glimpse of what the church is going to look like when the final curtain is pulled back. When God's Son speaks of *"wars and rumors of wars...nation [rising] against nation... famines, pestilences, and earthquakes"* (Matthew 24:6-7), you would think you are reading today's troublesome headlines.

Like me, you probably turn on the news and think, "I can't believe what I am hearing! It's just like the Bible predicts!"

Jesus gives us an insight into today's church by telling the story of the ten virgins.

Each one had been invited to a wedding celebration and instructed to bring their lamp. However, five arrived without any oil, and the other five came with barely enough—not a drop to spare.

We can see them waiting with excitement for the bridegroom, who was delayed. So exhausted, they fell asleep.

At midnight, a cry was heard: *"Behold, the bridegroom is coming; go out to meet him!"* (Matthew 25:6).

All ten rushed out to welcome him. Five had oil for their lamps, but the others had nothing. So those "without" said, "Give us your oil." They answered, "No. If we give you ours, we won't have enough. Go and buy some for yourself."

While out shopping, *"the bridegroom came, and those who were ready went in with him to the wedding; and the door was shut"* (verse 10).

When the groom arrived, he welcomed the five virgins who were waiting and prepared, then closed the door. Those without oil began knocking and shouting, "Let us in! Let us in!"

The bridegroom told them, *"Assuredly, I say to you, I do not know you"* (verse 12).

In the Middle East, weddings were a big deal—and still are. They celebrate for days, and sometimes weeks! Instead of just one reception, there can be five or six! Guests are eating and dancing nonstop!

For a bridegroom to be late because of a pre-marriage party was common. So when Jesus described the scene, it was in a cultural context Jewish people understood.

Scripture calls five of the virgins "wise," and the other five "foolish."

How many fell asleep? All ten! Even the five who had oil were unable to stay awake.

The point Jesus was making had to do with His return: *"Watch therefore, for you know neither the day nor the hour in which the Son of Man is coming"* (verse 13).

THE WRONG GOSPEL

This is a true depiction of the church today—fast

asleep. This can mean several things, including being distracted and not paying attention.

What is happening to us is easy to explain. Through the media, magazines, movies, and more, we have looked to the world as our role models and instructors. Sadly, we've bought hook, line, and sinker into a "feel good, self-help" gospel.

This was never meant to be. We have made ungodly exchanges with the culture, and now the world has influenced the church—instead of the other way around. Society has seeped into the fabric of how we think, breathe, and move. Millions have adopted the philosophy of, "I just want to be happy—and be my best me."

This is not scriptural. We are to be like Jesus! The best you can be is still rotten and sinful until Christ cleanses you from the inside out.

The church should not be driven by culture, the church should *drive* the culture!

DOES THIS DESCRIBE YOU?

There are three attributes that detail a courageous Christian:

Attribute #1: Alive!

The reason our spiritual compass is broken is because we remain silent and doze off—unable to recognize who we are and Who we serve. But the alarm bells are ringing all around us. God is warning, "Wake up!"

If you've been married more than five minutes you understand that a healthy, loving relationship requires your personal investment. This means more than paying the bills, raising the kids, and doing the chores.

A marriage that is simply functional and routine, is dead. There's no joy, no laughter, no consistency, no peace, no love.

The same is true with believers. If all we do is say the right words, show up at the right time, and play our role, our spiritual walk is lifeless. The vital connection with God is broken; there's no purpose and no passion. But the Lord has not called us to just a functional understanding of Him, but a vibrant, living, personal relationship.

I feel sorry for men and women who believe they will receive brownie points in the hereafter because of their good works here on earth. Unsaved people are generous, giving millions to the poor; sports heroes set up homeless shelters; celebrities fund foundations to cure illnesses. These are all laudable efforts, but unless a man or woman knows Christ, there is no eternal reward.

THANK GOD FOR RAIN!

During an extremely hot day at one of our kid's crusades in Mexico, it suddenly started raining. This wasn't just a sprinkle, but the heavens opened up. The downpour was so heavy that the water rose and covered the wheels of our van as we drove to the church. I thought we'd have to swim!

We finally made it—all 17 who were on our team. But no kids in sight.

About 30 minute after starting time, as we were praying together, a young, rain-soaked boy walked in. He was holding his little card—the printed invitation. Walking over to us, he asked, "Is it over?"

"No buddy, it's not," we responded, smiling.

"Can I come?" he asked.

Looking around at the team members, I could see the look on their faces, as if to say to that one small boy, "We're here for you." If we had traveled all this way for no other reason, it was for him.

We took him in, dried him off, and as we were giving the boy something to eat, a mother walked in with two little kids. They were drenched as well, and the woman said, "We are here because someone told me this is where I could find the real truth."

A total of six people finally showed up. We sat them in the front row and ministered from our hearts as if a thousand were present.

That day, six precious souls were added to God's kingdom as the rain of Christ's forgiveness flooded their souls. They were alive!

Attribute #2: Alert

Now is not the time to be swayed by emotion or the subtle pull of the things around you.

Some people are glued to social media or the news practically every waking hour and wonder why they are afraid and trembling. They don't realize that faith and fear grow the same way—by what we allow to enter our thoughts through sight and sound.

If you want faith to grow, fill your mind and heart with the Word of God. When you allow it to be your daily diet you will stay sharp and vigilant to everything the Lord is doing. Instead of contention and anxiety, you will have courage and assurance.

Allow the Bible to be your barometer. Just before telling the story of the wise and foolish virgins, Jesus declared, *"Heaven and earth will pass away, but My words will by no means pass away"* (Matthew 24:35).

If it is your desire to be alert and clear-minded, stay "wired" to the Word! Allow it to renew your thoughts, speak to your heart, and make you aware of the signs of the times.

Then, *"having done all...stand"* (Ephesians 6:13).

Attribute #3: Overflowing

How do we know we are living in the final hours? Even before Christ told us what to watch for during these last days, God spoke this through His prophet Joel: *"And it shall come to pass...that I will pour out My Spirit on all flesh; your sons and your daughters shall prophesy, your old men shall dream dreams, your young men shall see visions. And also on My menservants and on My maidservants I will pour out My Spirit in those days"* (Joel 2:28-29).

God is moving with might and dynamic power around this globe, reviving the church, and preparing the bride of Christ. We have been invited to the Marriage Supper of the Lamb (Revelation 19:9).

Is there oil in your lamp? Are your garments clean and white? Are you ready?

Perhaps you have only had a taste of God's blessing, and just a minor encounter with the Holy Spirit. Well, take it from one who knows: it's okay to be a little greedy when it comes to the favor of heaven. In these tumultuous days, "just enough" won't do.

Cry out to the Lord, "I want more! I long to live in the overflow of what You have for me."

Please don't be drowsy or distracted when the Bridgroom makes His glorious appearance. As a child of Almighty God, if you are not alive, alert, and enjoying the overflow, you are living beneath what God has planned for you.

A FINAL WORD

I want to personally thank you for spending this time with me. More important, it is my prayer that you will apply the principles and truths you have found on these pages to your daily walk.

- Decide to start living, instead of just breathing.
- Realize that you are designed for destiny.
- Awaken to life!
- Align your life with the supernatural.
- Remember that hunger is the key to increase.
- Dare to dream!
- Place your life on the altar.
- Never allow anyone or anything to steal your song.
- Open your eyes to God's miracle-working power.
- Become Spirit reflected and Spirit empowered.
- Make a commitment to being a courageous worshiper.
- Be alive, alert, and overflowing!

Please allow me to pray this prayer:

Dear Lord Jesus, I thank You for every reader and believe no one has read this book by chance or coincidence. I pray that each person would begin to live a truly courageous life without fear—and settle for nothing less than Your purpose for their future.

May you boldly pursue your divine destiny and have *The Courage to Live*—really live!